THE LOUVRE

The Louvre's bicentennial marks an important moment in the history of museums. The creation of the first French museum set out the principle of free access to the royal collections, which, saved from dispersion by the Revolution, thus became part of the national patrimony: on 18 November 1793, the gallery of the "Central Museum of the Arts" was definitively opened to the public.

This is a symbolic date for the creation of the modern state and for the conception of its patrimonial role and pedagogical mission that remains our own. This conception continues to justify the activity of the ministry that I now direct, which is, in André Malraux's words, "to make the outstanding works of humanity accessible to the greatest number of people."

What then is more natural for the Louvre's bicentennial than to offer the museum the possibility of expanding into the Richelieu wing, which, with the departure of the Ministry of Finance, now permits the Louvre palace to be entirely devoted to museum activities?

The museum that will be presented to the public has thus been profoundly transformed and renovated. But the operation is hardly completed. It will continue between 1994 and 1997. In the palace itself, the Cour Carrée and the Denon and Flore wings will be entrusted to young architects for remodeling and new presentations. Throughout the museum, technical and security facilities will be revamped. The renovation of the Union of Decorative Arts will also begin this year. The restoration of the facades will continue along the Carrousel gardens, on the Seine side, and in the Lefuel and Visconti courtyards.

But the Grand Louvre, to remain close to its history, must also involve itself with the Louvre and Tuileries Domain. I have insisted that the projects under study for the Tuileries and the Carrousel should be reviewed by the Higher Commission for Historical Monuments and the Sites Commission, as required by law. The observations that these two bodies have now made will be taken into consideration by the Public Authority for the Grand Louvre, which is responsible for the projects.

The restoration of the statuary, which is in poor condition, but also the replanting of the trees to guarantee the survival of the "Great Green Cover,"will be carried out with all necessary requirements and precautions. Likewise, the quality of the architecture for the garden concessions will be carefully examined.

This vast project has become meaningful through the exceptionally fine intervention of I. M. Pei, who has managed at one and the same time to respect the palace that is charged with seven centuries of French history and to introduce the modernity that is necessary to curators and public alike. I should therefore like to pay homage to him, for both the simplicity and the grandeur of his work.

For the past ten years, the programs carried out by the Public Authority for the Grand Louvre have focused on a domain of more than forty hectares extending from the Church of Saint-Germain l'Auxerrois to the Place de la Concorde. With the project that the city of Paris has entrusted to I. M. Pei for making the Place du Palais-Royal into a pedestrian mall, along with that for the reconstruction of the Solferino passageway, the public intervention is expanding and the Louvre palace opening even more onto its urban surroundings.

This ensemble, located between the Palais Royal and the banks of the Seine and connecting the Louvre Museum with those of Orsay, the Mint, the Legion of Honor, and the Orangerie, the Beaux-Arts Academy, and the Jeu de Paume Gallery, offers a concentration of history and culture without equal in the world.

Jacques Toubon
Minister of Culture and of the Francophone Community

p. 10

CONTENTS

This special issue of *Connaissance des Arts* marks the opening of the galleries of the Richelieu wing, a major step in the completion of the Grand Louvre project and one that coincides with the bicentennial of the museum's founding. It is intended as an invitation to discover these new spaces, but also to revisit the whole of the Louvre Museum.

The main participants in the project, curators and architects alike, have kindly offered their assistance for this issue, which has been jointly published with the Réunion des Musées Nationaux.

p. 22

p. 36

p. 44

p. 46

p. 54

FOREWORD

Year after year, readers of *Connaissance des Arts* have enjoyed detailed coverage of the Grand Louvre project, from I. M. Pei's first models to the completion of the Cour Napoléon and the Cour Carrée. Through articles, interviews, photo essays and special issues they have been able to follow the successive stages of excavation, construction, restoration, and the installation of the museum collections.

The phase that has now been completed, and which is the subject of this special issue, is decisive. With the opening of the newly restored Richelieu wing to the public, a vast ensemble of 178 rooms will finally permit the museum's collections to be displayed on the scale that they deserve.

As we know, the installations in the Cour Napoléon underneath the Pyramid were intended to provide the reception areas and technical facilities that were sorely needed. In the Richelieu wing, however, the works of art have pride of place. With the exception of the storage areas created under the courtyards and the workshops set up in the basement, the totality of the former Ministry of Finance has been allocated to the museum proper. Four departments—Sculpture, Oriental Antiquities, Decorative Arts, and Painting—benefit directly from this extension. It should not be forgotten, however, that the substantial enlargement of the space has also had positive effects on the other three departments—Graphic Arts, Egyptian Antiquities, and Greek, Etruscan, and Roman Antiquities—which have taken over the areas in the Sully and Denon wings that were vacated with the transfer of the other collections to the new wing. Thus, a vast, comprehensive reorganization of the entire museum has been carried out. The Richelieu wing was built by Visconti and Lefuel in 1852-1857 for the Ministry of State and other administrative departments. How exactly was its space redistributed? In fact, the process evolved rather naturally. It seemed wise to profit from the ample space and light of the three courtyards (Marly, Puget, Khorsabad) for the installation of the monumental sculptures that had originally occupied outdoor sites—parks, gardens, and public squares in France, the palace and its urban surroundings for Khorsabad. A chronological sequence of rooms devoted respectively to French sculpture and Mesopotamian civilizations could then radiate out from these courtyards. On the first floor, it was no less apparent that the Decorative Arts department should be located in the Napoléon III apartments, a setting that functions as a complement to the collection, bringing out the technical and ornamental richness of the different decorative arts. Finally, the top floor, which, as elsewhere in the Louvre, could be easily roofed in glass, was perfectly suited for paintings, which require overhead natural light. Conversely, the Islamic arts collection, notably the textiles and miniatures that are particularly sensitive to daylight, would adapt perfectly to the windowless areas of the basement.

Department by department, the pages that follow will show how the collections thus redistributed have been displayed, after a long collective effort on the part of the programming team, the architects, and the curators to define the precise sequence of the rooms, the placement of the partitions and display cases, and the location of each object. This overview brings out two essential elements. First of all, there are the architectural spaces devoted to specific ensembles—the monumental courtyards, the Medici Gallery, the Islamic crypt, the Maximilian and Scipio tapestry rooms, the rotunda with Poussin's *Seasons,* or the medieval treasury, to cite only a few examples—and these are so strikingly defined that the visual image of the place, like so many places in the Louvre, is as memorable as the work itself. But there is also the series of rooms—the galleries, the former artists' workshops with their northern exposure—that serve the timeless needs of the museum's collection. Visitors will appreciate the fact that the adaptation of the spaces to their new purpose, as deliberately contemporary as it might be, harmoniously integrates what remains of the building's architectural and decorative past—in this instance the reception rooms, the courtyards, the staircases. In fact, this has generally been the case at the museum since its creation two hundred years ago: I. M. Pei's great staircase echoes Hector Lefuel's, but also that of the *Victory of Samothrace.* For its bicentennial, the Louvre has received a new palace with a long history.

Michel Laclotte
President-Director of the Louvre Museum

1. *Winged woman on the prow of a ship, known as the* Victory of Samothrace, *marble (statue) and limestone (prow and pedestal), in the Department of Greek, Etruscan, and Roman Antiquities (h. 328 cm, c. 190 B.C.). Acquired in 1863 by the consul Champoiseau, this emblematic work, which is one of the museum's symbols, has crowned the Daru staircase since 1883.*

2

INTRODUCTION

The Public Authority for the Grand Louvre (EPGL) was created on 2 November 1983 with the mission of "conceiving and implementing the development of the Louvre and Tuileries Domain in order to make it an original cultural entity with a museum orientation, which will be known as the Grand Louvre, as well as permitting the integration of this ensemble into its environment."

Ten years later, to the day, the Louvre museum, enlarged by nearly thirty thousand square feet, is opening the Richelieu wing to the public and thus according I. M. Pei's project its full scope and logic. The Louvre Pyramid, the center of gravity of the collections, now assumes its role as the main reception area leading to the three wings of the Louvre palace: Richelieu, Sully, and Denon.

A parking lot with 650 places and a station for 80 buses now assure the museum's accessibility to vehicular transport, while an administrative garage for the personnel of the museum, the Council of State, the Constitutional Council, and the Comédie Française helps to reduce the number of parked cars in the area surrounding the Louvre palace.

The Place du Palais Royal, now given back to pedestrians, has become the forecourt of a museum that is generously opening itself up to the city after two centuries of discreet existence between the Seine and the Ministry of Finance. And in the process, the museum is revealing ever more of itself and its treasures.

The gardens of the Tuileries are also benefiting from the impact of the Grand Louvre all the way to the Place de la Concorde. The cultural perimeter, essentially focused on the Louvre, has thus been enlarged to include the Orsay Museum, the Jeu de Paume National Gallery, and the Orangerie, as well as the prestigious collections of the Decorative Arts Union and the adjoining Museum of Fashion. The world of fashion is also present in the Louvre-Tuileries area; located since 1986 in the Cour Carrée, this creative industry is now housed in the Louvre's Carrousel shopping mall, under the Carrousel garden.

The museum's dynamic cultural activity is becoming increasingly sophisticated in response to the multitude of visitors streaming to contemplate its world masterpieces, and this public now has ready access to services that permit them to eat a quick meal, to purchase gifts, and to profit from the time thus saved in order to visit the museums.

The Louvre palace, a historic monument that had been neglected for decades, is also gradually regaining its architecture, which is rich in sculptures and decorations accumulated under the impetus of five centuries of great French monarchs. The Louvre project has not been completed, however. The museum itself, extended into the Richelieu wing and the Cour Carrée, has to be modernized, rethought, restored, redistributed, reoriented around the Pyramid of I. M. Pei. The other parts of the palace will be transformed to house the curatorial offices of the Louvre, along with those of the Museum of Fashion or the Ecole du Louvre, and also the restoration workshops of the French Museum Administration. The palace itself, with its eleven hectares of facades and seven hectares of roofing, is due to be entirely restored, as are the gardens in and around the Louvre.

All of this work will bring us to 1997, the date when the EPGL will cease to exist. Its responsibilities will then be passed on to those in charge of the facilities created within the framework of the Grand Louvre project, beginning, of course, with the Louvre Museum, which has also had the status of a public authority since January 1993 and which will obviously have the responsibility and the desire to continue this vast cultural enterprise.

The phase that has come to an end today is essential, however, and I would sincerely like to thank all of those who have worked on this project for the past ten years: architects, engineers, technicians, administrators, contractors, workers, artisans, and artists, as well as the curators and personnel of the Louvre Museum.

Jean Lebrat
President of the Public Authority for the Grand Louvre

2. *The museum's extension into the Richelieu wing, built during the Second Empire, has also provided the occasion for renovating the facades and restoring the exterior sculptures.*

FROM PALACE TO MUSEUM

Inaugurated by the Convention in 1793 as the Central Museum of the Arts, the Louvre Museum was closely tied to the spirit of the Enlightenment. It fell squarely within a vast movement that saw the peoples of Europe raising questions about their past and demanding broad access to royal collections. Two centuries after its founding, the Louvre remains in the vanguard as an illustration of the most recent advances in contemporary museum science.

The Museum's Beginnings

While the Central Museum of the Arts was clearly a product of the Revolution, it would be unfair to give the revolutionaries all the credit for this innovation. Indeed, years of reflection preceded the opening; it was at the end of the seventeenth century, with the departure of the royal court

3. *Jan Van Eyck's* Rolin Madonna *(wood panel, 66 x 62 cm), which entered the Louvre in 1800, was confiscated from the Collegiate Church of Notre-Dame in Autun.*

4. *The first works to enter the Louvre were those from the king's collections, such as Caravaggio's* Fortune-Teller *(o/c, 99 x 131 cm), presented to Louis XIV in 1665 by Prince Don Camillo Pamphili.*

to Versailles, that the Louvre's orientation began to shift from politics to art.

Abandoned by the court, the palace was to become the fief of the academies and the artists. The Academy of Painting and Sculpture, meanwhile, was to leave the Hôtel de Brion for the Louvre in 1692. From 1751 on (following a series of initial attempts in 1699, 1704, and 1725), exhibitions of its members' works were held twice a year—apparently the first signs of the palace's new vocation. Workshops and apartments for painters and sculptors that were installed by Henri IV on the ground floor and entresol of the Grande Galerie soon extended to the palace and the ramshackle cottages around it. Indeed, not only was the building neglected, but even more so its surroundings: groups of shanties and scaffolding invaded the courtyards and the colonnade conceived by Claude Perrault to such an extent

that there was a public outcry. In 1745 and again in 1749, Voltaire protested the "shameful state" of the Louvre. Similar arguments proliferated. In Diderot's *Encyclopedia*, his 1765 article on the Louvre similarly called for the complex to be transformed into a temple of arts and sciences housing painting collections in the Grande Galerie and a museum of sculpture, as well as the artists, on the ground floor.

The king could hardly turn a deaf ear to such insistence. In 1754, the architects Gabriel and Soufflot were delegated to restore the colonnade and complete the courtyard facade of that wing. This marked the beginning of the destruction of the shanties blocking the courtyards. With public finances disrupted by the Seven Years War, the project slowed down and finally came to a halt for lack of funds. During the same period, there was a strong demand for the display of the royal collections, not so much to present them to the "general public," but rather to make use of them for the training of artists. In October 1750 the government made a partial concession to this request: 110 paintings from the royal collection were exhibited at the Luxembourg Palace. This proved to be only a temporary solution, however, for in 1779, the Luxembourg was

5. *During the Italian campaign of 1797, the army, under the direction of a committee of scholars, plundered museums, private collections, and churches. This* Crucifixion *(wood panel, 76 x 96 cm) comes from the predella of an alterpiece commissioned from Andrea Mantegna (1431-1506) for the Church of San Zeno in Verona.*

6. Christ and the Children *by Sébastien Bourdon (o/c, 50 x 61 cm), acquired by Napoléon Bonaparte in 1801, photographed here in the French painting section on the Cour Carrée.*

granted to the king's brother, the count of Provence.

At that time the count d'Angiviller, director of the Buildings Administration, was promoting a project for a French museum in the Louvre and to that end ordered the relief plans of the kingdom's fortresses to be transferred to the Invalides in 1777. A commission was assigned to study the crucially difficult question of the lighting in the Grande Galerie. The Academy of Architecture recommended installing overhead apertures, reinforcing the wooden roofing, and providing it with partitions of fireproof brick. Seeking to avoid further procrastination, d'Angiviller announced in November 1788 that as an experiment, for the next exhibition in August 1789, the Salon Carré would receive overhead lighting. In a report, he noted that the failure to carry out the various projects was due not so much to France's financial difficulties as to technical questions.

The Central Museum of the Arts

What the Ancien Regime was not able to undertake, the Revolution succeeded in carrying out. On 26 May 1791, the Louvre and the Tuileries were officially allocated "to the king's living quarters, to the regrouping of all the monuments of the Sciences and the Arts, and to the main institutions of public education." After the fall of the monarchy on 10 August 1792, the commission assigned to organize the museum saw its mission enlarged: it was now to gather paintings from the royal residences and the possessions of emigrants and the Church for the Louvre. Thus in 1794 the Louvre was to receive Michelangelo's *Slaves* and Mantegna's *Allegories.* Van Eyck's *Rolin Madonna,* removed from the collegiate church in Autun, was also retained.

If the museum's collections were quickly enriched, the construction work advanced slowly. In order to move it along once and for all, the Convention decided—on 27 July—that the first anniversary of the fall of the monarchy would be marked by the opening of the "Museum of the Republic." This was wishful thinking, however: notwithstanding a hastily improvised inauguration, visitors were only admitted to the palace on 18 November.

The museum's main objective was the instruction of artists. Thus, out of the ten-day week instituted by the Revolution, five days were reserved for painters and sculptors, two for the work of the conservatory and three for the public.

Stripped of the royal insignia, the Grande Galerie now displayed for the edification of all some 137 paintings—excluding romantic and pastoral scenes that were judged too titillating and relegated to Versailles, where a special museum for the French School was opened in 1797. The works displayed (without labels!) were grouped by school, regardless of periods or genres. The presentation was complemented by 124 objects, including three astronomical pendula, installed on tables.

The sorry state of the buildings required another closure. Only a selection of paintings remained visible in the Salon Carré. During the same period, the museum underwent an unprecedented expansion. As had already been the case in Belgium, the army, under the direction of a committee of savants including Monge, Berthollet, Gros, and Moitte, now brought back from Italy a selection of interesting "objects of the arts and sciences."

It was in this way that the *Belvedere Apollo,* the *Laocoon,* and the *Medici Venus* entered the Louvre, temporarily at least. These plunder operations also yielded Giotto's *St. Francis* and Raphael's *Marriage of the Virgin,* which Paris, "city of the arts," welcomed with a victory parade.

In addition, the property of emigrants continued to be confiscated. Portions of the Choiseul-Gouffier collection, including a section of the Panathenaic procession from the Parthenon frieze, were deposited in the Louvre in 1798. Thus, when the museum was partially reopened in 1799, and even more so after Bonaparte and Joséphine had sumptuously inaugurated it on 9 November 1800 (18 Brumaire of the year IX according to the revolutionary calendar), the collections were considerably expanded.

The masterpieces of the foreign schools (643 paintings, now organized by school) lined the Grande Galerie, which was enlivened with figure busts on tall marble columns. The antiquities, meanwhile, were installed in the former summer apartment of Anne of Austria, on the ground floor.

The Musée Napoléon

In November 1802, Bonaparte, now installed in power and conscious of the importance of the museum and the prestige it could bring him, decided to reform its administration. Different collections and artistic departments were thus placed under the responsibility of a general administration headed by the chevalier de Non, known as the imperial baron Denon under the Empire. Aiding him in his task were the architect Dufourny, appointed curator of the paintings, and especially Ennio Quirino Visconti, who, as director of antiquities, imbued the Antiquarium with his personality. The Central Museum of the Arts, which became the Musée Napoléon in 1803, enjoyed tremendous renown throughout Europe.The refurbishing of the palace, entrusted to the

7

architect Pierre Fontaine, was intended to improve access to the museum and free it of cumbersome annexes. All the artists who still had studios and apartments in the Louvre were relocated to the Capuchin convent, while the workshops along the colonnade and the shanties in the Cour Carrée were demolished.

More important, Napoléon called upon Charles Percier and Pierre Fontaine to revive the program of the kings, namely the joining of the Louvre and Tuileries palaces. A series of proposals ensued, but the project came to nothing for lack of a clearly defined approach. Other construction was nonetheless undertaken. The Empire was to complete the Cour Carrée and the facade on the Seine. Fontaine built the Carrousel, which, marking the entry to the Tuileries courtyard and recalling Napoléon's victories, extended the north wing from the Marsan pavilion along the newly built Rue de Rivoli.

THE LOUVRE: KEY DATES

1180 Accession of Philippe Auguste, who initiates construction of the Louvre.

1364-1380 Charles V makes the Louvre his residence and has the ramparts extended.

1546 François I calls on architect Pierre Lescot and sculptor Jean Goujon to reconstruct the building in the Renaissance style.

1563 Catherine de Médicis commissions Philibert de l'Orme to build a palace on the domain of the Tuileries located outside the ramparts.

1610 On the death of Henri IV, the Louvre and the Tuileries are joined by a gallery along the river.

1643 At the end of Louis XIII's reign, construction is begun on the Cour Carrée.

1667 Construction of the colonnade by Perrault.

1715 On the death of Louis XIV, the Cour Carrée is completed, work on the colonnade begun, and the small gallery restored.

26 May 1791 The Louvre is assigned to the "regrouping of all the monuments of the sciences and the arts."

18 November 1793 The Central Museum of the Arts opens to the public.

1810 The north gallery is constructed along the new Rue de Rivoli.

1852 Napoléon III commissions Visconti to join the Louvre and the Tuileries in order to create a vast museum-palace complex.

1861-1865 The west part of the Grande Galerie and the Flore pavilion are rebuilt by Lefuel; the Louvre carriage gates are created.

1871 A fire rages through the Tuileries, which is demolished ten years later. The Ministry of Finance moves into the Richelieu wing.

1968 The Flore wing is returned to the museum.

1981 President François Mitterrand gives the Richelieu wing, known as the ministers' wing, to the museum and subsequently places I. M. Pei in charge of an ambitious project to create a Grand Louvre.

1989 The Pyramid marking the museum entrance is inaugurated. □

7. The scholar Jean-François Champollion was the first curator of the Egyptian section, created in 1826. This statue of the «Divine Consort» Karomama, dating from the twenty-second dynasty (bronze inlaid with gold, silver, and black and white paste, h. 59 cm) was one of his acquisitions.

8. This Apollo (bronze, h. 115 cm, second half of the fifth century B.C. ?), found in the sea near Piombino, was purchased during the rule of King Louis-Philippe (1830-1848).

8

The Museum of Louis XVIII and Charles X

Given its close association with imperial policy, the Louvre naturally suffered the consequences of Napoléon's downfall. The countries that had been deprived of their property sought to recover it. In 1814, only Prussia and the German principalities managed to have a number of works restored to them. After Napoléon's defeat at Waterloo, Italy also made vociferous claims on its paintings, sculptures, and art objects. In the absence of any directive, Denon vigorously defended his collections, with the result that a hundred paintings, notably retables from the thirteenth and fourteenth centuries, were abandoned by the Florentines, and an exchange between a Le Brun painting and Veronese's *Wedding Feast at Cana* was negotiated. More than five hundred works were shipped back to Italy, however, including the horses of St. Mark's and 106 marbles from the Borghese collection.

In order to make up for this impoverishment, Louis Forbin, who succeeded Denon as director of the "royal museums," demanded the sixteenth- and seventeenth-century works held by the Museum of French Monuments, which was to close its doors in June 1816 after the property of emigrants had also been restored. Several gifts (such as the famous *Venus de Milo* given to the king by the marquis de Rivière), purchases of contemporary works (David's *Sabine Women* and *Leonidas at Thermopylae,* Géricault's *Raft of the Medusa*), and deposits (Vernet's *Ports of France,* Le Sueur's *Life of St. Bruno,* and Rubens's Marie de Médicis cycle were transferred from the Luxembourg) helped to round out the collections.

In 1824, five new rooms were opened between the Clock pavilion (pavillon de l'Horloge) and the Beauvais pavilion; these formed a suite called the Angoulême Gallery, which housed 94 sculptures, many of which were recent works commissioned by Napoléon I. The nucleus of a future sculpture department, this section was part of the Department of Antiquities created in 1802 and basically included everything that was not painting or drawing.

This department was to undergo a spectacular development under Charles X. In 1825, Edmes Antoine Durand sold the Louvre his collection, which included a thousand antiquities as well as more than five hundred objects (enamels, ceramics, and stained-glass windows from the Middle Ages and the Renaissance). Three years later, the painter Pierre Revoil, a former pupil of David and classmate of Forbin, ceded his collection of medieval and Renaissance objects, furniture, ivories, tapestries, and enamels.

Charles X's museum was further distinguished by the creation of an Egyptian section, the first of its kind. In 1826, Jean-François Champollion, the historian and linguist who succeeded in decoding Egyptian hieroglyphics, became its director, and a series of extraordinary acquisitions was added to the rare pieces that the museum already owned. Thus Champollion purchased in a single lot the four thousand pieces of the collection assembled by Henry Salt, the British consul in Cairo. Between 1827 and 1833, Fontaine (who had been successively reappointed by Louis XVIII and Charles X) set up four galleries in the south wing of the Cour Carrée in order to exhibit these works.

During the July Monarchy (1830-1848), Fontaine was likewise delegated to install the Spanish gallery. Inaugurated in January 1838 on the second floor of the Colonnade wing, it

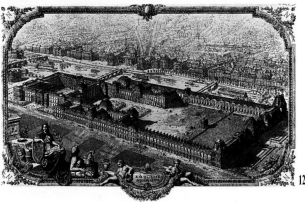

included 450 paintings acquired for Louis-Philippe by Baron Taylor. Unfortunately, as the personal possession of the king, this collection was restored to him after his fall and dispersed in London in 1853—undoubtedly one of the Louvre's gravest losses, since the museum is still rather poor in the area of Spanish painting.

Louis-Philippe was also responsible for the creation, on a permanent basis this time, of the museum's first Oriental section. In 1847, Paul-Emile Botta, French consul in Mosul, sent back to Paris the fruits of the excavations conducted on the site of Khorsabad in Iraq.

At the dawn of the Second Empire, the museum spread into the four wings of the Louvre's Cour Carrée. Barely one month after the 1848 Revolution, the provisional government ordered the resumption of work on the building, beginning with a thorough emptying of the space. Félix Duban and Philippe Jeanron, superintendent of the palace and director of the museum, respectively, arranged for the renovation of the facades of the small (Apollo) gallery, and the Seven Chimneys room and the Salon Carré were refurbished and adapted to the taste of the day.

The Second Empire and After

With the Second Empire, the Louvre was to enter a period of prosperity that saw the completion of the great project long favored by the kings and never carried out by the Empire. In 1852, Napoléon III directed Ludovico Visconti (son of the curator of antiquities under the First Empire) to connect the Louvre with the Tuileries and to remove "the eyesores that disfigure the facades" so that this monumental ensemble might house the palace of the sovereigns, the offices of the administration (telegraph, press, barracks), ministries, and a museum.

Respectful of the monument and its history, Visconti hoped that "the character of the new architecture would be religiously borrowed from the Old Louvre," and insisted that "the architect will sacrifice all of his pride in order to preserve for this monument the character that his predecessors have imparted to it." In order to mask the displacement of the Louvre-Tuileries axis and the differences of levels between the quay and the area around the Carrousel, Visconti planned to articulate the space by means of courtyards. He also envisioned lengthening the gallery built by Fontaine along the Rue de Rivoli, which was itself to be extended. The construction of two buildings with interior courtyards allowed the service areas for the royal court to be extended along the north and the museum along the south. Thus, for the first time in the history of the Louvre, a building specifically intended to serve as a museum was added to the palace. In the center of this new edifice was the Denon pavilion, which included a main entrance on the ground floor and new galleries. With a genuine concern for exhibition needs, the latter were provided with high moldings and overhead lighting, and particular care was given to the decor.

With the death of Visconti in December 1853, Hector Lefuel assumed responsibility for completing the project and in the process, introduced a more complex and copious ornamental scheme. In record time, after only five years of work, the new palace-museum ensemble was inaugurated by Napoléon III on 14 August 1857. Shortly afterward, Lefuel rebuilt the Flore pavilion and by 1866 completed the Louvre carriage gates on the Seine facade of the Grande Galerie.

9. 10. *One of Hubert Robert's favorite subjects, the Grande Galerie can be seen here as it was between 1801 and 1805 (o/c, 37 x 46 cm) and as he imagined it with overhead lighting (33 × 42 cm).*

11. *Conscious of the prestige that the Louvre Museum could bring him, Napoléon consciously associated it with the major events of his rule. Benjamin Zix,* Wedding Procession of Napoléon and Marie-Louise, *2 April 1810 (pen and ink with sepia and bistre highlights, 40 x 60 cm).*

12. *It was Napoléon III who finally managed to accomplish what the kings had aspired to before him: the joining of the Louvre and the Tuileries (engraving by R. Pfnor, 1853).*

Next double page:
13. The Battle of San Romano, The Counter-Attack of Michelotto da Cotignola *(wood panel, 182 x 317 cm), by Paolo di Dono, known as Uccello (1397-1475), comes from the extraordinary Campana Collection, which was acquired in 1861 and entered the Louvre two years later.*

These enlargements mainly benefited the Painting department, which was greatly in need of space by that time. In 1862, a hundred fourteenth- and fifteenth-century panel paintings were deposited in the Louvre following the acquisition of the marquis de Campana's collection; in addition to the paintings, the former director of the municipal pawn-brokerage in Rome owned an extraordinary collection of Greek ceramics and remarkable Etruscan pieces. In 1869, through the La Caze donation (the largest in the Louvre's history), major works of eighteenth-century painting were finally exhibited in the Louvre.

During the same time, the Department of Antiquities developed considerably as the finds from excavations conducted by French archaeologists in the East were sent back to the museum. In 1852, August Mariette's campaigns in Sakkara revealed the necropolis of the Ancient Empire and enriched the Egyptian collection with the Apis divine bull sculptures. In 1860 Ernest Renan deposited the remains discovered in Lebanon, and in 1863, the archaeologist Champoiseau sent back the *Victory of Samothrace*. Decorative arts gradually made their way into the museum as well. From 1861 on, the Apollo Gallery, decorated by Delacroix in 1850-1851, received semiprecious stones, metalwork, and enamels in specially designed display cases that are still in place. The rest of the collection was presented in eight galleries on the first floor of the Cour Carrée's north wing.

When Franco-Prussian War broke out, the interior renovations were not yet completed, but even more than the war, it was the tragic days of the Commune that were to threaten the Louvre-Tuileries complex. The Tuileries went up in flames. The blaze spread through the Flore and Marsan pavilions as well as the adjoining galleries, but it was limited to the height of the carriage gates through the efforts of devoted personnel led by the curator, Joseph Barbet de Jouy. Lefuel quickly undertook the restoration of the pavilions and galleries. The fate of the Tuileries was to remain in suspense for ten years before it was finally demolished in 1881.

It was thus necessary to wait an entire century for the whole of the Louvre palace to become the Louvre Museum. The Central Union of Decorative Arts was the first to benefit from the spaces left vacant. In 1877, a museum was set up in the Flore pavilion, prefiguring the Museum of Decorative Arts that was to be inaugurated in the Marsan pavilion in 1905. The Hall of States, meanwhile, was to revert to the museum in 1886 after Edmond Guillaume, Lefuel's successor, provided it with a skylight. It was then used for the display of late eighteenth- and early nineteenth-century French painting. At the same time, the Salle du Manège (the former riding school) was given to the Department of Greek and Roman Antiquities, which, following the arrival of the first traces of Sumerian civilization in 1881, was separated from the Department of Oriental Antiquities.

After a period of dormancy, the States pavilion, vacated by the municipal council in 1883, reverted to the museum. The architect Blondel, newly appointed to the palace, provided sumptuous decorations for the gallery where Rubens's Marie de Médicis cycle was to be installed.

The collections developed and acquired greater autonomy as the century came to a close. In 1893, sculptures were separated from decorative arts. Eight years later, the

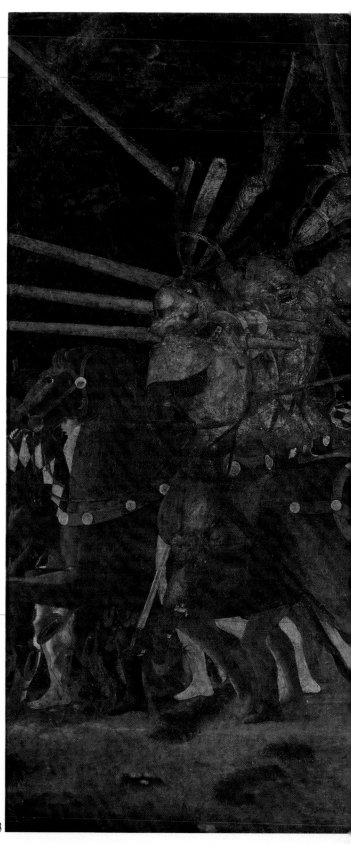

13

Department of Sculpture, benefiting from a decree that gave it a good number of pieces formerly in storage, spread out over five new galleries located on the first floor of the Cour Carrée's west wing. The museum next turned toward the Flore pavilion: the collection of nineteenth-century bronzes and paintings donated by Alfred Chauchard was installed on the first floor in 1910. After the departure of the Ministry of the Colonies, the rest of the pavilion was annexed by the Ministry of Finance for the National Lottery administration.

For lack of space, different departments spread out somewhat haphazardly in the palace. Thus, after the Second World War, the new director of the National Museums, Henri Verne, initiated a remodeling program that was completed in 1948. Verne intended to reorganize the departments and redistribute the space. He had passages constructed in the basement so that visitors could circulate continuously on

14.

14. *Throughout the Second Empire, excavations undertaken by French archaeologists in Egypt, Greece, and the Middle East brought the Louvre first-quality antiquities, such as this* Seated Scribe *(painted limestone, h. 53.7 cm, Old Kingdom), found by the Egyptologist Mariette in the Sakkara cemetery.*

15. *Ordered in 1821 by the Count de Forbin, who was at the time the Director of the Louvre, this «Hercules and the Serpent» by François-Jospeh Bosio was originally placed in the Tuileries palace. It is now exhibited in the Cour Puget.*

the ground floor. A reception room was then set up in the Salle du Manège, which now had great bays overlooking the Cour Napoléon and the Seine. Similarly, in order to facilitate the public's visits, the Daru staircase and the Mollien staircase were enlarged and completed.

It was only in 1961 that then-Minister of Cultural Affairs André Malraux was able to have the Flore wing returned to the museum. And it was only in 1981, with the decision of newly elected President François Mitterrand that the Louvre could envision extending its collections to the Richelieu wing. With the Ministry of Finance transferred to Bercy, the architect I. M. Pei was able to propose an ambitious project finally providing the museum with adequate structures to receive its public. Inaugurated in 1989, Pei's Pyramid has become the symbol of the Louvre and its modernity.   V. L. B.

15

Italian Painting

16. *Commissioned for their refectory in 1562 by the monks of San Giorgio Maggiore in Venice, this* Wedding Feast at Cana *by Paolo Caliari, known as Veronese, entered the French collections in 1798 (o/c, 666 x 990 cm).*

17. *Another example of the seizures carried out by imperial troups in Italy is Giotto's* St. Francis of Assisi Receiving the Stigmata, *which came from the Church of San Francesco in Pisa (wood panel, 313 x 163 cm).*

18. *This portrait of the writer and diplomat Balthazar Castiglione (1478-1529) by Raphael already graced the royal study of Louis XIV, who purchased it from the heirs of Cardinal Mazarin upon the latter's death in 1661 (o/c, 82 x 67 cm).*

19. *Upon the death of Leonardo da Vinci, King François I acquired the works left in the master's studio, including this* Virgin and Child with St. Anne *(wood, 168 x 130 cm).*

Next page:
20. *Sometimes attributed to Giorgione, the* Concert Champêtre *is a key work from Titian's youthful period. With a subject that has never been clearly defined, it remains one of the most mysterious paintings in the Louvre (o/c, 105 x 136.5 cm).*

21. *Between 1766 and 1770, Francesco Guardi executed twelve paintings on Venetian festivities. Among the ten that belong to the Louvre is this* Doge Attending the Maundy Thursday Festivities on the Piazzetta *(o/c, 67 x 100 cm).*

16

17

18

19

ANTHOLOGY

The opening of the Richelieu wing should not completely steal the scene from the hundreds of masterpieces exhibited in the Louvre's other galleries. A selection follows.

23

22

20

23

21

24

French Painting

22. The Cheat with the Ace of Diamonds *is one of Georges de La Tour's finest daylight paintings. Discovered in 1926, it was acquired by the Louvre in 1972, the year of the first retrospective devoted to the Lorrainese master (o/c, 106 x 146 cm).*

23. *Like Nicolas Poussin, one of France's greatest seventeenth-century masters, Claude Gellée, known as Claude Le Lorrain, spent nearly all of his career in Rome.* The Disembarkation of Cleopatra at Tarsus *(o/c, 119 x 168 cm).*

24. *Presented at the Salon in 1742, this* Diana at the Bath *is one of the most famous paintings of François Boucher, who was granted a studio in the Louvre in 1754 through the efforts of Mme de Pompadour (o/c, 56 x 73 cm).*

25. *This portrait known as* The Writer *by Jean Honoré Fragonard is one of the works that Dr. La Caze bequeathed to the Louvre in 1869 (o/c, 80.5 x 64.5 cm). Behind this painting, photographed during the installation of the Cour Carrée galleries, can be seen a portion of Jean-Baptiste Santerre's* Susanna and the Elders *(o/c, 205 x 145 cm).*

25

27

26

28

29

26

26. *Antoine Watteau's* Gilles, *also bequeathed by Dr. La Caze, belonged to one of the most important figures in the history of the museum, Baron Vivant Denon, durector of the Musée Napoléon (o/c, 185 x 150 m).*

27. *King Louis-Philippe was the owner of this painting recalling the revolutionary days that brought him to power.* Liberty Leading the People (28 July 1830) *by Eugène Delacroix (o/c, 260 x 325 cm).*

28. *One of the masterpieces of the great Neoclassical painter Jacques Louis David,* The Sabine Women *(o/c, 386 x 520 cm).*

29. *This painting, probably Théodore Géricault's most famous work, was so violently criticized when first presented at the 1819 Salon that the count de Forbin, director of the Louvre Museum at the time, could not have it acquired, despite his own enthusiasm.* The Raft of the Medusa *(o/c, 491 x 716 cm).*

30. *View through a window overlooking the Cour Carrée, photographed during the installation in 1992.* The Valpinson Bather *by Jean-Auguste-Dominique Ingres (o/c, 146 x 97.5 cm).*

31

32

33

34

Department of Graphic Arts

31. The Department of Graphic Arts, which boasts more than 180,000 items in its collection, contains such major works as this Portrait of Isabella d'Este *by Leonardo da Vinci (pierre noire, red chalk, pastel, 63 x 46 cm).*

32. The collection of the Cologne banker Eberhardt Jabach, forcibly turned over to Louis XIV, included among its drawings this View of the Val d'Arco, *one of Albrecht Dürer's rare landscapes (watercolor and gouache with pen and black ink, 22.3 x 22.2 cm).*

33. *The Louvre owns three admirable self-portraits in pastel by Jean Siméon Chardin (45.9 x 37.5 cm).*

34. *The consulting room of the Department of Graphic Arts was installed on the upper landing of the old monumental staircase in the Flore wing. Visible on the tables are drawings by Nicolas Poussin.*

Department of Decorative Arts

35. *This clock in gilded and patinated bronze is decorated with a porcelain plaque dated 1826 and representing Gen. Foy, leader of the liberal opposition during the Restoration. The plaque appears to have been painted by Marie-Victoire Jaquotôt.*

36. *Mme Récamier's bed, the archetype of the Empire bed, was made by the Jacob family of cabinetmakers around 1798.*

37. *Charles X's bed in the Tuileries, by Pierre-Gaston Brion. The silks from Louis XVIII's bedchamber were adapted to the bed provided for the new king in 1825.*

Department of Sculpture

38. 41. *Michelangelo conceived the* Captives *(also known as the* Slaves) *for the second version of the tomb of Pope Julius II. The Louvre owns two of the sculptures that he began executing. To the right, a detail of the* Dying Slave *(marble, h. 228 cm), and on the opposite page, the* Rebellious Slave *(marble, h. 209 cm, detail).*

39. *Antonio Canova's* Eros and Psyche *(55 x 68 x 101 cm, seen here in detail), completed in 1793, was acquired by Gen. Murat.*

40. *This* Virgin of the Annunciation *by Tilman Riemenschneider had an angel, probably kneeling, as its pendant (alabaster, partly gilded, h. 53 cm)*

38

40

39

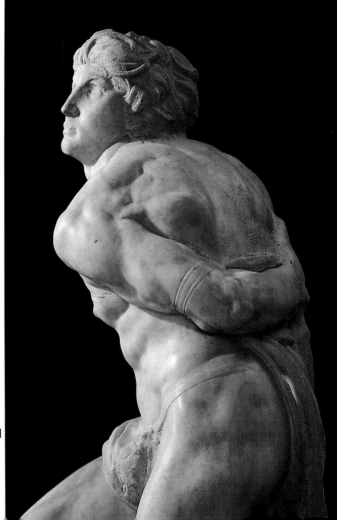

41

Department of Egyptian Antiquities

42. *Tutankhamen returned to the traditional religion after the Amarnian revolution led by Amenophis IV (Akhenaton) and swore allegiance to the god Amun. Here the young pharoah is shown at the feet of the god, who is given his features (diorite, h. 214 cm, c. 1347-1337 B.C.).*

43. *Egypt donated one of its colossal statues of Amenophis IV to France to express its gratitude for French participation in the rescue of the Nubian monuments in 1972 (painted sandstone, h. 137 cm, c. 1365-1349 B.C.).*

44. *Discovered in the masonry of the tomb of Nefertiabet (the daughter of Cheops?), this funerary stele shows the deceased surrounded with the food and cosmetics that she would have needed in the afterlife (painted limestone, h. 37.5 cm, c. 2575 B.C.).*

45. *A bust of Tutmosis IV, grandfather of Amenophis IV, photographed in the galleries (pink granite, h. 75 cm).*

46. *This* Sarcophagus of a Married Couple, *a major work of Etruscan art discovered in Cerveteri, was part of the Campana Collection (terra cotta, h. 114 cm, late sixth century B.C., detail).*

47. *The Cyclades have yielded a range of Early Bronze Age figurines, from simple circles to life-size statues. This fragment probably belonged to full-size example (marble, h. 27 cm, c. 2700-2400 B.C., found on Keros).*

47

48. *Found in Hera's sanctuary on Samos, this statue offered as a gift to the goddess is one of the first* kore *from eastern Greece (marble, h. 192 cm, c. 570 B.C.).*

49. *This funerary stele from Thessaly, known as* The Exaltation of the Flower, *shows two women facing each other with flowers and bags of grain (?) in their hands (marble, h. 60 cm, c. 460 B.C.).*

50. *This head probably belonged to a colossal bronze statue of the emperor Hadrian, reflecting the prosperity of his reign (h. 43 cm, second quarter of the second century A.D.).*

46

48

49

50

35

FOR A NEW MUSEUM

Because of the positions they occupy, Michel Laclotte and Jean Lebrat were called upon to oversee the conception of the new Louvre. They explain how this ambitious project was developed.

Connaissance des Arts: Could you tell us how it was decided to include the Richelieu wing within the Louvre Museum?

Jean Lebrat: It all goes back to a declaration by President Mitterrand in 1981, where he asked his prime minister to look for a site for the construction of a new Ministry of Finance so that the whole of the Louvre palace could be allocated to museum activities. It was this decision that launched the entire Grand Louvre operation.

CdA: Wasn't the decision the result of a request from the museum's curators?

Michel Laclotte: The request had been under the surface for several generations. You have to remember that in the early 1930s the director of the national museums, Henri Verne, was studying a large project that included the taking over of the Ministry of Finance offices, and even the use of the Cour Napoléon. The question was revived after the war and again in the 1960s, when André Malraux, the French minister of cultural affairs, was thinking about it. For the Louvre it was something obvious; it was a hope for us, but clearly impossible without a government decision. This Richelieu wing offered the only possible extension for a museum that was suffocating. The priority had always been the presentation of the works, which is normal, but the public reception areas were, to say the least, not all that could be hoped for. It's not easy to install checkrooms or cash registers, for example, in a palatial setting.

CdA: It could be said that this Grand Louvre project for a museum was developed on the basis of a political decision.

JL: Yes, you could say that, in the good sense of the word *political*.

CdA: Jean Lebrat, you're the head of the Public Authority for the Grand Louvre [EPGL], but the Louvre Museum itself now has the status of a public authority, which headed by Michel Laclotte. How are the activities of these two structures related?

JL: The Public Authority for the Grand

51. *The Cour Napoléon with its newly restored facades and sculptures.*

51

Louvre is a body that was created to carry out the project, and it will cease to exist when that project is completed. It's a temporary public authority with a very precise mission on the terrain of the Louvre and the Tuileries, which relates to the palace, its interior design, and the transformation of administrative offices into museum spaces, but also the immediate surroundings of this palace, so that it will have the best possible connection with the city around it. If the EPGL is responsible for the project on the qualitative and financial levels, and for the deadlines, it also has to make sure that the projects that have been carried out under its responsibility suit those who are to use them. This is, I think, what brought out the essential role of the museum in the necessary dialogue between the EPGL and the user, whose identity is thus naturally reinforced as the project evolves.

ML: For our part, when we began to implement the project, we didn't really envision this status of public authority. We had obtained the creation of a specific administration for the museum, dependent on the French Museum Administration. That allowed us to incorporate a certain number of departments, such as the cultural department, for example, directly into the Louvre, and to create others. It was only when all of that was put in place and began running normally that we felt the need for greater autonomy in management. That had been anticipated by some and contested by others, and it required a painstaking examination. We thus worked very closely with the French Museum Administration as well as the Réunion des Musées Nationaux [Union of National Museums, RMN], in order to find an original formula for a public authority that would suit what the Louvre Museum is now as well as what it will be later, when the EPGL will no longer exist. But it's only an administrative transformation, which completely maintains the Louvre in the family of national museums, notably with regard to personnel and acquisitions policy—unlike the Pompidou Center. One more important point: the president and director of the museum are one and the same person, and we managed to establish—this was an essential condition—that this person would always be a curator. The function of the other curators remains unchanged.

CdA: Doesn't this transformation imply

greater responsibility in the area of management and possibly that of the museum's "profitability"?

ML: We already had these preoccupations before. Let's say that from now on, handling a budget that's clearly identified in its expenditures and its revenues will make things clearer, more transparent.

CdA: Let's come back to museum

53

issues. Will the vast increase in area that the Richelieu wing brings to the museum be accompanied by an equal increase in the collections displayed?

ML: No, the area is doubled but there's no question of doubling the number of works presented. What we wanted above all was a better presentation. Nonetheless, many works are coming out of the storage areas. Just look at what there is for French sculpture, around the *Horses of Marly*. And the Islamic art collection, which had hardly been shown, now has thirteen galleries, which allows for a real chronological presentation. And in fact, indirectly, this expansion will lead to what

52. The spiral staircase under the Pyramid, which provides the main access to the reception areas.

53. Leonardo da Vinci's celebrated Mona Lisa, *acquired by King François I after the artist's death, attracts an ever-increasing public. The new location of this masterpiece in the Grande Galerie will make it more accessible (wood panel, 77 x 53 cm, c. 1503-1506).*

54. 55. *The Napoléon III apartments formerly belonging to the Ministry of Finance are now open to the public (on the first floor of the Turgot pavilion). Their lavish decoration is one of the most striking examples of the Second Empire style.*

is practically a general reorganization throughout the Louvre. When everything is finished, the only parts remaining from the pre-Richelieu state will be the Greek and Roman classical sculpture galleries that were remodeled a decade ago—with a new presentation for archaic Greece and the pottery—and the large red rooms for French painting, which are separate from the French painting section recently opened around the Cour Carrée. Egypt will change entirely, as will the Oriental collection outside the Richelieu wing.

CdA: What's striking about these new installations is a very clear predilection for spaciousness. Does this decision stem from the architects, the curators, or the EPGL?

ML: The three-way agreements were the best, but you know, the architecture itself imposed these spaces that the architects have retrieved or created. Some of them were clearly readable on the facade—where there were offices piled up on two levels, all that could be seen was a high window.

CdA: You were never tempted to gain space by adding storeys inside?

JL: No. More often the problem was just the opposite. It was necessary to find museum spaces in a building conceived from the outset for the departments of the Ministries of the Interior and the Post Office. Aside from the large Napoléon III halls, the rest was occupied from the beginning by offices, with entresols and internal partition walls containing the original chimneys. The confrontation between respect for the cultural heritage and the indispensable transformations linked to the integration of a museum was delicate. I would even say that one of the reasons for the creation of a separate Public Authority was precisely the need to find a structure somewhat outside the institutions. It was out of the question to ignore the legitimate mandate of the Direction du Patrimoine [Cultural Heritage Adminstration] to intervene in the building. The mission of the head architect for historical monuments, responsible for the domain, was defined from the very beginning. But the Public Authority for the Grand Louvre could call on other architects, a situation that expressed the particular nature of the operation. While it was quite certain that *Maximilian's Hunts* could not be placed in the old offices, various elements were preserved when the space adapted itself to the museum's use.

With the exception of the large halls and the monumental stairways, obviously. The concern for preserving the cultural heritage is manifest, moreover, in the major effort of restoring the facades and the roofs, which was naturally entrusted to Guy Nicot, head architect for the palace.

CdA: In creating this expansion project, have you proceeded to readjust the relative importance of the various departments of the Louvre?

ML: Clearly there was the extreme case of the Islamic arts, which were notoriously under-represented. But while we carefully studied the different programs, I have to say that the readjustments, the arbitrations, were not so difficult. Some things were obvious. Painting needs natural overhead light, so the top floor was reserved for it. The ground floor is better for the weight of the sculptures. The textiles, miniatures, and precious objects of the Islamic arts flee daylight and thus were well suited to the basement, for example. And it was logical to link the Napoléon III apartments with the Decorative Arts department on the first floor. Once it had been decided that sections such as the restoration workshops, the laboratory, and the Ecole du Louvre would be packed off to the outer fringes that the Flore wing had now become, because of the reorientation created by the Pyramid, and that the sculpture leaving this wing would be installed in and around the Marly courtyard, all the rest followed rather easily.

And there are plans everywhere, more detailed ones than what is given out with the purchase of a ticket.

CdA: Do you think that the opening of this wing helps to change the circuits that draw large crowds, to diversify them?

ML: The only thing we know is that there will always be lots of people in front of the *Mona Lisa,* wherever we put it. But Richelieu, like all novelties, will certainly attract people for a certain time. The attraction of the large Napoléon III halls, of the Marly, Puget, and Khorsabad courtyards, the new Medici Gallery, and the new rooms that could be called the "medieval treasury" will play a large role. And then the great escalator, which leads directly to the paintings, will also provide a strong incentive.

CdA: Does the distribution of the great masterworks, the high points, fit into a strategy of tour circuits?

ML: We never wanted to place the key

56

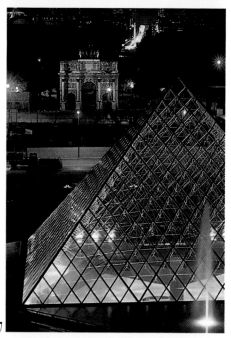

57

58

works in such a way as to permit a rapid tour of the Louvre. They've been placed where they should be in a chronological sequence, perhaps with a nuance for the *Mona Lisa,* which is slightly out of place.

CdA: When the Pyramid was opened, there was talk of a desire to change the nature of the public, or at least to influence its visiting patterns, to increase the length of these visits. What has happened since?

ML: First of all, we've already extended the Louvre's visiting hours: it's open from 9 a.m. to 6 p.m., and twice a week until 10 p.m. This is hardly the case for most museums! As for the average length of a visit, you know, there's a natural limit—at the end of two or three hours, fatigue sets in. Knowing and attracting publics is something we do by various methods, notably by considerable activity on the part of the public relations and cultural departments. We are seeing a gradual increase in the proportion of the Parisian public, or that of the greater metropolitan area, which traditionally came to the Louvre one time and never returned. More broadly, a long-term effort is being made in relation to the French public. The activities of the auditorium, for example, are hardly aimed at the passing tourist who only spends one or two hours at the Louvre. And we do want to diversify our public.

JL: The shopping areas will also attract people, and the architectural arrangement should naturally encourage them to take a look at the museum side. Everything connects easily. But also, with the opening of Richelieu, the museum becomes like a window on the Rue de Rivoli, toward the city. From the outside, one sees the inside, the galleries all lit up, through the large windows and the openings on the courtyards. That doesn't resemble any other museum.

CdA: Are you hoping for an increase in the total number of visitors?

ML: We really don't know, and we have to be very cautious. At present there's a slight decline in the number of entries all over the world. Nor is a massive new increase the main goal of the project. We already welcome nearly five million visitors a year! But obviously, given the fact that the exhibition areas have doubled, even if we receive a million more visitors, the flow of the public will generally be smoother, and the visit itself will be more pleasant.

Interview conducted by
Philip Jodidio and Denis Picard

56. 57. Two exterior views of the Pyramid.

58. These enamels by Bernard Palissy (c. 1560-1570) were discovered during the excavations of the Cour Napoléon. They probably came from the decorations of the grotto of the Tuileries, which was built by Catherine de Médicis.

59. The Venus de Milo, another museum celebrity, draws the admiration of dozens of visitors every day (marble, h. 202 cm, c. 100 B.C.).

43

ARCHITECTURE

I. M. Pei, with his associates, played a central role in determining the new master plan of the Louvre. The importance given to architecture in this instance is significant, and the considerable problems encountered in creating a modern museum in an historic palace have been decisively resolved. By Philip Jodidio.

With the support and encouragement of the French government, in 1993, the Louvre accomplished the task that had been set forth two centuries before. The opening of the Richelieu wing, and of the commercial spaces in the Carrousel area completed the essential aspects of the «Grand Louvre» project that began to take shape in 1983. With the Pyramid and the associated underground spaces, opened in 1989, the museum gained essential infrastructure such as adequate reserves, restaurants and an ample bookshop. The Carrousel passage added not only an innovative commercial space, but a long needed underground parking lot for cars and buses. It was the addition of the Richelieu wing however, with 22,000 square meters of new exhibition space which finally confirmed the transformation of the Louvre Palace into a museum, a change which had begun when the institution opened to the public in 1793. It was a decision of François Mitterrand, the President of France, to liberate the North wing of the palace, long occupied by the Ministry of Finance, and to relocate the Ministry, with its 5000 employees to the Bercy area in the East of Paris, which permitted the development of a new master plan for the museum.

60

French administration is highly centralized, so a Presidential decision on matter of this nature is essential to making rapid progress. François Mitterrand called on Emile Biasini, a former head of French Television and member of André Malraux's cabinet to head up the Louvre project, and he determined, in part on the basis of the National Gallery's East Wing, which the architect had completed in 1979, that I.M. Pei would be the best designer possible. It seemed obvious that the eight, cramped and low-ceilinged floors of the former Ministry of Finance would have to be removed and replaced by ample spaces which would permit thousands of works of art to be put on display, some for the first time in many years.

A New Entrance for the Louvre

As Yann Weymouth, Designer-in-charge of the initial phase of the project explains, in order for this new space to be of use, "two other components would be needed: a new

60. 61. *A considerable importance was given to the presence of natural light in the Richelieu wing. To the left, a view of one of the Northern School galleries on the second floor shows the overhead lighting system designed by I. M. Pei and his associates. Complementing the natural light, artificial sources are concealed by the cross-like blades. To the right, the Inverted Pyramid in the Carrousel zone marks the completion of the Grand Louvre project by I.M. Pei, and echoes the Pyramid in the Cour Napoleon.*

entrance, as the existing entrances were already inadequate to handle the numbers of visitors, and the technical infrastructure that nourishes a modern museum, such as secure storage areas, laboratories, and even adequate public restrooms, which did not previously exist in the Louvre." It was I.M. Pei, during three secret visits to the museum before he officially accepted responsibility for the project, who determined that the entrance, and indeed the new infrastructure spaces would have to be centrally located in order to properly serve the three wings of the museum, Denon, Sully, and the new Richelieu wing. In an interview published by *Connaissance des Arts,* Pei likened the underground spaces he planned to the lower, vital decks of a ship. Through the use of stone and certain design elements, the new Louvre would appear to be an organic whole, into which the underground areas woud be integrated in a natural and conclusive way. The apparent aspect of the first phase, the Pyramid was necessary in order to signal the entrance of the Museum, but also to give an ample, generous feeling to spaces which were below grade. Again in *Connaissance des Arts,* Pei explained that the great French garden designer Le Nôtre had called on water and sky as elements for his creations. The Pyramid, surrounded by fountains, reflecting the changing sky, would, in a way, be an homage to Le Nôtre.

The Pyramid was to generate a large amount of controversy, especially after the conservative daily *Le Figaro,* took position against it. During an essential meeting, organized by Emile Biasini at Arcachon in January 1984, the curators of the Museum, among them Michel Laclotte, who subsequently became the director of Louvre, came together with the architects and issued a joint statement of support for the project. This, together with a mock-up, which gave an indication of the size of the completed pyramid, turned the tide of opinion. The remarkable coherence and architectural quality of the project, as evidenced in the completed Pyramid, and related underground spaces are ample proof, not only of the success of I.M. Pei's visionary design, but also of the impressive work of the architectural team. Michel Macary was involved in the project from the outset, and Pei's partner Leonard Jacobson was a key personality for technical design questions. Without "Jake", who has since passed away, the Grand Louvre project might not have been what it is. For the design, Yann Weymouth, Andrzej Gorczynski, Stephen Rustow, Masakazu Bokura and several others created the multitude of details which set this project apart.

The very coherence of the Grand Louvre project was called into doubt in 1986 when, with a change in government, it became apparent that the Ministry of Finance might not after all leave the Richelieu wing. In the course of a luncheon with François Léotard, then Minister of Culture, and

see page 50

RESTORING THE MUSEUM'S PALATIAL DIMENSION

An interview with I. M. Pei and the other architects who have participated in the Richelieu project.

CdA: How was it decided that it was necessary to completely empty the Richelieu wing, apart from the historic areas, as opposed, for example, to keeping some of the interior floors?

I.M. Pei: To begin with, the Richelieu wing was occupied by the Ministry of Finance. The place inside was actually a rabbit-warren of offices with no large spaces. So there was no disagreement among any of us. It was a natural decision.

Stephen Rustow: In fact, the original structure was built in 1850-1860 with the entresols, because it was conceived as a government office building. What was paradoxical, of course, was the rhythm of the façades, which gave the impression that the building had only three floors whereas it always had more. Our decision in some sense was to give the nineteenth-century building the spaces that it always pretended to have had behind the façades, but that it never had. We decided to make it like the rest of the Louvre, to integrate its interior into the palatial volumes of the older areas.

Michel Macary: It was built for the Post Office administration for one, and also that of the Ministry of Finance. There was also the governmental Pension Fund. Monumental architecture of that period always included entresols except where there were reception rooms. The decision to hollow out the Richelieu wing was made at the beginning of the project, in the context of the draft master plan in 1983.

IMP: Before the Grand Louvre project, the Louvre was actually a wall, eight hundred meters long, separating the Right Bank from the Left Bank. Our idea was to open the Passage Richelieu that leads from the Place du Palais Royal to the Pyramid to the public.

MM: One of the advantages of the Passage Richelieu is also that it lets the public have a view over the courtyards into the museum below. In the Passage

62. One of the most remarkable spaces of the new Richelieu wing in architectural terms in the escalator, with its spectacular round openings, designed by I.M. Pei. The attention of Pei and his assistants to details is visible in every aspect of this area.

Richelieu, people can immediately see down into the museum, without even having to go inside.

CdA: One of the things that strikes me very much about the spaces above grade in Richelieu is how generous the galleries are. It is striking for modern architecture—because this is naturally modern architecture—that you have such ample space. There are not many new spaces anywhere in the world that have this kind of generous feeling.

IMP: It's a great luxury. It is of palatial scale, and that was, I think, used to great advantage. Curators usually want more space, but here, not one of them suggested introducing entresols.

CdA: I'd like to ask a question about the division of responsibility between the architects. How was it decided who would take care of each space? Mr. Pei, we talked about your role as coordinator [*mandataire commun*], but how was it decided, for example, that M. Macary would be responsible for the sculpture areas?

IMP: It became quite clear, after the Pyramid was accepted and con-

63. 64. The transparency of the architecture in terms of both the light and the openings that permit visitors to orient themselves, was a priority for the architects. To the far right, one of I. M. Pei's original drawings for the Louvre (1983), showing the access to the three wings of the museum.

structed, that this project had to move on to the second phase, in which the involvement of French architects became essential. As for the Pyramid itself, and the underground space, which is not small, the responsibility was strongly on our side, there is no question about it. Michel Macary was selected to assist me at that time. There was some concern that a new competition be avoided, so they came out with this Solomonic solution, to say, I. M. Pei, maybe you can continue as a *mandataire*, or as a coordinator. It's not a role I like, but at that time I acquiesced, and I said this is the right way to go to the second phase. When Wilmotte's name was mentioned, and he was already a collaborator, I felt that it was natural that he participate, so the team was formed in this fashion. Pei, Cobb, Freed's role, or my role actually, was the following: we have had a general overview of the plan itself, with such important decisions as the location of the escalators. The prolongation of the plan from the Cour Napoléon all the way into the palace, I would say, was our role, but in addition to that we have also done

the top floor. It was my decision to let Stephen Rustow take over the Khorsabad courtyard and the Oriental Antiquities, so we had a very good team from the very beginning.

SR: There was never any question of a single architect or a single team of architects doing the whole of the Louvre.

CdA: But is such a division of responsibilities the best solution for the quality of the architecture?

IMP: I think it was necessary, because first of all we're dealing with an existing building, not designing a new one. Secondly, it involved very complex dealings with curators, so I think the decision to accept to partition it in that fashion was a very wise one.

MM: In the beginning we thought that it was very important to see the installation process through to the end, while the EPGL [Public Authority for the Grand Louvre] felt that this was more the domain of the curators, that we were supposed to provide empty rooms that they would organize afterward. In practice it became clear that there was a relationship between the way of displaying the works and the designing of the rooms themselves, right down to the choice of colors, which was thus a very important and lengthy process.

CdA: Has it been possible nonetheless to maintain the unity of the whole?

MM: I think that the unity of the coloring appears more through the intensity of the tones. On every floor, there's an unusual variety of intense colors.

Jean-Michel Wilmotte: The overall use of oak flooring is very important for the unity, as are the display cases, and the lighting.

IMP: I think there was very strong preference on the part of the owner, the EPGL as well as ourselves to give coherence to this, in spite of the fact that many hands were involved and many curators—giving Jean-Michel Wilmotte, for instance, all the display cases is one example—so there is a unity. All the public circulation areas, like escalators, are treated in the same way.

CdA: One difficulty has always been the movement of visitors through the Louvre. With the addition of the Richelieu wing, haven't you in fact complicated the visit?

IMP: I don't think so. The Louvre is probably the biggest museum in the world,

and for this size collection, I think it's now quite coherent.

CdA: Isn't it too big?

IMP: The Louvre is not intended to be visited in one day, and this is one of the main reasons that the Pyramid was put in. The underground connection created a cross with three museum destinations: Denon, Sully, and now Richelieu. The project has simplified movement within the museum despite adding extra space. We now have an infrastructure in this museum, which it badly needed. When we first analyzed the old museum, the percentage of infrastructure support was less than 10 percent. In all the modern museums that have been built recently, the proportion is closer to 50 percent. So one of our great contributions was therefore to build enough infrastructure for reserves, for conservation—.

CdA: To make it a modern museum.

IMP: —for public amenities. Restaurants, cafés, this kind of thing, was never considered by the management of the Louvre until we came along. Even the

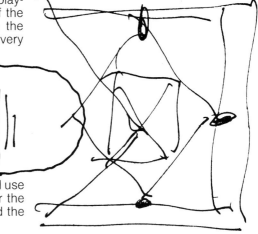

64

Louvre bookshop is a very important adjunct, which was not accepted by many who ran the museum in the past. The entry, the coherence, the circulation, the identification of the three wings, are very important to the identity of the museum. In the end, I would like to say this, that historically, traditionally, the Louvre Museum has consisted of seven separate entities. Each department is, so to speak, its own principality, and one of the great contributions of this particular enterprise is that for the first time, under the able, tactful leadership of Michel Laclotte, we see the emergence of a single Louvre. □

continued from page 46

Edouard Balladur, Minister of Finance, in June 1987, I.M. Pei convinced the new government that the Richelieu wing was critical to the concept the museum.

Given the extensive work required on the historic parts of the building in the Richelieu area, Guy Nicot, the Chief Architect of the Louvre became directly involved. It was decided for various reasons that I. M. Pei would become the coordinator or *mandataire commun* of the second phase with Michel Macary handling the ground floor sculpture areas, Jean-Michel Wilmotte the first floor Decorative Arts department, and the Pei team for the public circulation spaces such as the spectacular escalator, the lower level Islamic arts section, the Oriental antiquities department on the ground floor, and the top-lit galleries for paintings on the second floor. this phase naturally required close cooperation between architects and curators. Since Emile Biasini became Minister for the *"Grands Travaux."* in 1988, he was replaced at the head of the Public Authority for the Grand Louvre by Jean Lebrat.

Four Goals for the Richelieu Wing

As Yann Weymouth points out, the architectural team worked on a four-part scheme, whose goals in the Richelieu wing were to: "*Save* all historically important elements, all of the exterior, facades, roofs, and inside, the three great staircases and the Napoléon III apartments.

Remove the rest of the interior, all small, low-ceilinged offices, all nonessential interior walls.

Create a new museum wing within the shell, with spaces scaled to the works to be contained, appropriately lit either from the great windows or from skylights above, always respecting the historic facades and the tissue of the existing museum to which Richelieu would be attached.

Insert all the services, security systems, air-conditioning, fire safety, and the elevators and escalators needed for public and private circulation.."

Although the space in the Richelieu wing is vast, a certain number of galleries will undoubtedly retain the attention of the public. Since the escalator leads visitors naturally up to the third floor, and since paintings do constitute the core of the collections of the Louvre, many will begin their visit there.

One of the main reasons that the Paintings Department was placed on the second floor during the discussions at Arcachon, was to take advantage of the natural overhead lighting. Because mechanical systems which vary the amount of light admitted tend to break down rather easily, I.M. Pei's team opted for a non-mechanical set of grilles designed to bring light onto gallery walls, as opposed to the floor where it tends to fall. An elegant cross-like design on the ceilings permits artificial light to supplement the outdoor source as required. In every aspect of these rooms, from the lighting itself to the finishing of the details, the quality of the work of Pei and his associates is evident.

Moving down one floor, the Decorative Arts Department was handled by the architect and interior designer Jean-Michel Wilmotte, who is also responsible for all of the display cases in the new area. Here, darker colors on the walls seem to blend more easily into the rich assemblage of objects which form one of the finest collections in the world of its type. Visitors will undoubtedly retain the enormous Maximilian gallery with its cycle of tapestries and display cases of majolica as one of the high points in the new

65. *A view of the Marly courtyard.*

66. to 72. *Next double page: This series of images, to the left, shows the Pyramid and the related underground areas. To the right, a spectacular photo taken by Alfred Wolf of the newly restored facades of the Louvre, with Paris in the background.*

65

spaces. Here, as elsewhere, the visitor feels the "palatial dimension" of the architecture, which seems natural in the Louvre, but which in fact did not exist in this area before 1993. Subtle and perfectly in harmony with the work of I.M. Pei, Wilmotte confirms his reputation here as one of the leading French designers.

The ground floor areas were the work of Michel Macary for the Sculpture Department, and Stephen Rustow (Pei Cobb Freed) for the Oriental Antiquities. The visitor will certainly be most impressed by the three internal courtyards, baptized Marly, Puget and Khorsabad. It should be emphasized that these courtyards served as parking lots for the Ministry of Finance. A good part of their transformation lies in the construction of the skylights which were designed by the engineer Peter Rice. The Marly and Puget Courtyards, containing French sculpture, are divided by the Richelieu Passageway which leads at ground level from the Pyramid to the Palais Royal. Visitors thus enter these spaces from the lower level, and must go up seven meters to reach the ground floor. The massing of architectural elements in these areas is thus a combination of curatorial requirements and the necessity to bring people up one level. The Khorsabad Courtyard, designed by Stephen Rustow, is not as large as the other two, but deals well with the complex problem of evoking an historical location (the Palace of Sargon II) without delving into excessive historicism.

On the lowest level of the Richelieu wing, Stephen Rustow has made what will undoubtedly be a lasting contribution to the architecture of the Louvre by creating a series of low-ceilinged rooms which serve for the display of Islamic art. Although the Louvre boasts a large collection of Islamic art, it had never before been displayed.

Here, in an atmosphere of appropriate mystery which maintains the necessary architectural continuity with the other areas of Richelieu, a marvelous variety of objects await discovery.

Through the use of certain materials, through the treatment of the public circulation spaces, such as the elegant and spectacular well for the escalator in the Richelieu wing with its two enormous round openings, the architects have given this new space a feeling which is at once contemporary, and yet somehow intimately related to the palatial past of the Louvre. This in itself is a testimony to the mastery of I. M. Pei, and of the other architects.

The Carrousel and the Inverted Pyramid

Another new space certainly deserves mention, although it is not technically part of the Louvre Museum. The passageway and commercial gallery leading from the underground parking lots to the Pyramid also blends in a harmonious, indeed spectacular way into the new Grand Louvre. Designed largely by Michel Macary and Gerard Granval these spaces have at their center the wonderful inverted pyramid, which brings light into the lower level while accenting the continuity of these spaces with the Louvre. Its amazingly light structure was designed by Pei and his associates, including the late Andrzej Gorczynski together with Peter Rice and RFR. In itself it is a fitting end to a visit of one of the most important architectural accomplishments of the late twentieth century. The Grand Louvre stands not only as a tribute to French culture, but to the men and women who succeed in transforming a palace into a truly modern museum.   P. J.

RICHELIEU FROM TOP TO BOTTOM

It's the new face of the Louvre: with its 4 levels, 6 collections, 178 rooms, and several thousand works of art spread over some 22,000 square meters, the Richelieu wing is like a museum within a museum and one that sets the tone of what the Grand Louvre will be when it's done. By Denis Picard.

Have you tried to imagine what it means for a museum to open so many exhibition galleries, not to mention the corridors between them and the numerous service areas? And all the choices that such an installation calls for?

Even when the spaces were distributed in the best possible way relative to the general nature and specific requirements of the collections involved, the vast wealth of these collections still left curators with an infinite number of choices, granted that these entailed the acceptance of a first, determinant choice: that of giving the maximum exposure to all of this wealth. As far as the general outlines are concerned, it is easy for the experts in the trade to select one possible arrangement among others. But in the details, installation becomes a real exercise in gymnastics, one of the most subjective of arts, and at the same time, a kind of game of dominos in which there are hundreds, if not thousands, of pieces (all of which have to be kept in mind) that have to go together not only because of what they are and the strategy of the game, but also in function of external elements such as space, volume, light, or color. In terms of color, the new Louvre confirms a revival of colored walls. Here too there are objective conditions to be met, but ultimately, it comes down to the greatest subjectivity, which accounts, for example, for the obvious difference between the pastels of the French painting galleries and right next door, the intense hues of the Northern schools. The uniform treatment of the corridors, entrusted to a single architect, I. M. Pei, provides one unifying element. Another comes from the range of display cases proposed by Jean-Michel Wilmotte but even so, there are nearly 70 different models for the 575 individual cases concerned.

In the end, all of that adds up to fine, beautiful, even very beautiful French museum, and before long, it will not be hard to see that the Richelieu wing makes the other galleries of the "old Louvre" a little obsolete, if not totally antiquated. But rest assured, a renovation is anticipated, and if it is a must to inspect the magnificent contribution of this new opening, it will also be a must to come back in 1996 or 1997, when the Grand Louvre will be totally completed—if such a museum can ever be "finished."

73, 74. This portrait of Jean le Bon *is the work of an anonymous artist, painted on wood panel (60 x 44.5 cm, c. 1350). It is the first work in the French paintings section, at the top of the escalator in the Richelieu wing. In the image to the left, the contrast between the colors of the rooms for the Northern schools in the background (green) with that of the French rooms is visible. In the foreground, a concert scene by Valentin de Boulogne, and a view toward a second room with works from the Fontainebleau School.*

Next page:
75. This majestic hanging of works by the painters of Louis XIII centers around canvases by Simon Vouet and Philippe de Champaigne (portrait of Richelieu).

74

73

What French Painting is About

For French painting, the Richelieu wing is almost a culmination—but one that starts at the beginning, because what is involved is linking the seventeenth century to the very first attempts at easel painting, and the new itinerary begins, significantly, with the *Portrait of Jean le Bon* (c. 1350). For a number of galleries, the addition of the Cour Carrée is (relatively) modest, with the contribution of Richelieu—to the Northern schools, for example—much more noteworthy. But this expansion gives the French School a great opportunity. The galleries renovated by Italo Rota in 1992 suffered because of their isolation and all the stairs that had to be climbed to find them on the second floor (and what floors!). From now on, thanks to the Richelieu wing's imposing escalator it is possible to get from the Pyramid to the beginning of the section in some sixty seconds. And the nineteen additional galleries, which go from the top of this escalator around the Khorsabad courtyard to the corner of the Cour Carrée, also provide the opportunity to take another look at the installation carried out in a dozen galleries to the north of the Cour Carrée in 1989.

76

The choice of the second floor for the painting collections was a given because of the possibility, in practically all the galleries, of obtaining the natural overhead light that is so conducive to the proper viewing of a painting. This light, moreover, is now subtly controlled, by means of a cross-shaped device on the ceiling, so that it just skims over the painting without harming it. And of course, it is helped along with hidden artificial light sources that compensate for overly large fluctuations.

On the floor, a light parquet bordered with a narrow strip of stone that matches the baseboards marks a no-man's-land for visitors, reiterated for greater safety by thin barriers. The walls offer a range of off-whites in shades of gray-beige, pink, cinnamon, and champagne, and sometimes more intense hues such as the reddish plum of the little end room that provides an intimate setting for the delicate portraits by the Clouets and Corneille de Lyon. This soberly refined setting thus permits the rediscovery of the adventure of French painting from the modest likeness of Jean le Bon all the way to the imposing royal celebrations of a Charles Le Brun. The installation still follows a chronological order but permits a few large groupings—of painters or genres—that mark

77

76. 77. 78. Simon Vouet Allegory of Wealth, (o/c, 170 x 124 cm), Claude Vignon The Young Singer, o/c, 95 x 90 cm), Lubin Baugin Still Life with Wafer Biscuits, a work presented in the newly rehung rooms of the Cour Carrée, (oil on wood panel, 41 x 52 cm); three masters of the seventeenth century, which was, perhaps even more than the eighteenth century a golden age of French painting.

high points in the section quite apart from the presence of a certain well-known Louvre masterpiece. Thus we go from the school of Burgundy to that of Provence for an encounter with the inevitable *Avignon Pietà* by Enguerrand Quarton (c. 1455). Then come Jean Fouquet, the Master of Moulins, something new with a painting by Jean Perréal, who was not previously exhibited at the Louvre, the graceful Mannerism of the first School of Fontainebleau, the followers of Carravagio (Valentin de Boulogne, Claude Vignon), the painters of Louis XIII, Simon Vouet, Jacques Blanchard, and Philippe de Champaigne. Poussin finally receives the full honors he deserves in three entire galleries (with Claude Lorrain), offering a dazzling combination of *Christ and the Woman Taken in Adultery, The Judgment of*

78 *Solomon, Diogenes,* the celebrated *Self-Portrait* (1650),

see page 60

57

PAINTINGS, COLORS, AND CURATORS

An interview with Pierre Rosenberg, head curator, Department of Painting.

Connaissance des Arts: What were the criteria for installing a large part of the Paintings department in the Richelieu wing?

Pierre Rosenberg: Of all the large museums, the Louvre is perhaps the only one that can claim an encyclopedic vocation and display painting in its universality. That is reflected in the presentation of both the greatest possible number of painters and entire spectrum of genres history painting, religious and mythological painting, portraits, genre scenes, still lifes. So it could be said that we didn't really have a choice to make—we had to show our collection to the fullest extent, bringing

CdA: The choices that you have to make don't depend solely on the works. They imply questions of lighting, decoration, architecture, security. As a curator, where do you stand in all of that?

PR: Today's curators are in fact expected to have more and more competences. They are supposed to be scholars, administrators, and managers all at once! Personally, I believe that the great curator is the one who knows best how to study, preserve, and publish the collections he or she is in charge of, and above all to expand them. It seems that this kind of curator is becoming a rare species, a dying breed. It's an international phenome-

79. 80. *The new French painting section in the Richelieu wing gives a place of honor to Nicolas Poussin. Several rooms permit an understanding of the evolution of his work (such as the* Et in Arcadia Ego, *o/c, 85 x 121 cm, detail), with a final round room in which his* Four Seasons *are displayed (left).*

79

everything possible out of the store-rooms.

CdA: But even so, in the display of ''everything,'' there were still many choices that presented themselves.

PR: Of course. That of the chronology, for example. And that of preserving the grouping by major schools: the French, the Northern schools, two areas affected by the opening of the Richelieu wing, also Italy. And also, as I've said, that of bringing out the different genres. Of course, in the details, every element of the installation is the result of an accumulation of little choices: a particular combination of works, of artists.

non, and one that I can only deplore.

CdA: But at the same time, the curators here have been able to benefit from the know-how of many teams of specialists, technicians, and architects with whom they've developed a close collaboration.

PR: Certain questions came under the domain of the curators, others, that of the architects. And between these two ''reserved'' areas, there were free territories. That was the space for dialogue, where each person had to know how to listen to the other one without losing sight of the only goal: to serve the works in the best possible way.

80

The curators had requests concerning, for example, that basic question of overhead natural lighting. The problem was to limit the influx of light in summer and conversely to get the most of it in winter, all by means of the same device. It was up to the architects and lighting designers to resolve this problem of squaring the circle, and up to us to judge the result. For the artificial lighting, the specialists proposed different systems. It had to be one of the best possible quality, but not too sophisticated, so that it would work on a day-to-day basis. And there, for example, the curator really had to know how to judge. In such areas, where the quantity of technical know-how has considerably increased, the competence required of the curator grows proportionately.

CdA: The new galleries mark a return to colored walls. Does this mean the advent of a new era in museum science, after that of the ''modern'' grays and whites, or is it a return to certain conceptions from the last century?

PR: You know, there's no absolute truth in this area, no hope of unanimity. It's a question of taste; whatever the choices, there will always be something to criticize. We've tried to find colors that bring out the paintings, without excess and without competing with them, but we know very well that the issue is not settled forever. To be sure, the atmosphere is darker than the one that prevailed in the 1970s; the time of the antiseptic hospital wards, so to speak, is over.

CdA: There's also a return to a dense installation.

PR: Yes, but that's not done in the spirit of a return to the nineteenth century. The installation in these new galleries is in fact tighter than before. But perhaps the very airy style of hanging the works, with one painting per wall, came to us from the US, where this was done for a certain time because there was nothing left to put on the walls.

CdA: In this gigantic redeployment, as well as in the different approaches that can be observed between the French and the Northern galleries, how does your responsibility as department head work?

PR: I wanted to leave a great deal of freedom to my team of curators, while intervening like an orchestra leader who makes sure that his musicians play correctly: the parts are different for each instrumentalist, but the overall score is the same.   □

81

81. 82. *This masterpiece by a very well known artist, the* Self-Portrait *by Dürer (1493, oil on parchment on canvas, 56.5 x 44.5 cm) and an anonymous masterpiece, the* Pietà *by the Master of Saint-Germain-des-Prés (97.3 x 198.5 cm, right) surrounded by works by the Master of St. Séverin and by the Master of St. Bruno, are a few examples of the wealth of the German paintings collection of the Louvre.*

Following double page:
83. 84. *One of the high points of the galleries devoted to Northern schools is this group of Rembrandts, with two 1663 self-portraits, the* Holy Family, Philosopher in Meditation, *and other works. Another seventeenth-century Dutch master, Frans Hals is represented by this* Bohemian Girl *(o/c, 58 x 52 cm, left).*

and many other masterpieces leading up to the *Four Seasons,* the moving late works that have been given a spacious rotonda to themselves.

The tour of the Richelieu wing ends here. But by extension, this installation has permitted the renovation of thirteen additional galleries around the Cour Carrée. As if to crown its slow reinstatement, the great religious painting of the seventeenth century holds pride of place, notably with the rediscovery of Eustache Le Sueur's *St. Vincent* series. Also rediscovered, at last, within the galleries now allotted to the great Parisian decors, the reinstallation of the Hôtel Lambert paintings. The still-life galleries, the La Tours, and the Le Nains remain in place. And we can end up with the Marengo pavilion, where the reinstallation of the large-format works of Champaigne and Le Brun (the *Battles*) in summer 1993 preceded the reorganization of the entire early French painting section.

The Colors of the North

Coming back to *Jean Le Bon* but turning left this time, we arrive at the beginning of the large section devoted to the Northern schools. Spread over some forty galleries around the Puget and Marly courtyards and punctuated with high points like the Medici Gallery, this is an astonishingly rich ensemble, and its rigorously intelligent presentation makes no concessions to the effects that might have been permitted by the presence of such masterpieces as Jan Van Eyck's *Rolin Madonna,* Dürer's *Self-Portrait,* or Vermeer's *Lacemaker.* With sobriety and discretion, they all somehow come back into line in a very tight installation that often aligns the paintings on two levels, combines large and small formats, mixes genres (still lifes and portraits, landscapes and genre scenes), and ultimately restores the pictorial effervescence of the era in both the diversity of its

NORTHERN LIGHTS

The galleries devoted to the Northern schools benefit from the force of unity by virtue of the fact that they were entrusted to a single architect and decorator, namely I. M. Pei. And they are all the more important because they constitute the first direct intervention within the museum itself on the part of the person whose Pyramid had defined and symbolized the new Grand Louvre. The Pei rooms on the second floor of the Richelieu wing were intended to avoid the difficulties encountered by the rooms on the same floor of the Cour Carrée. Like the latter, they benefit from the overhead lighting that is a privilege of the top floor, but reject the principle of flat skylights in favor of a system of arches and half-domes that add height and a feeling of spaciousness. The rooms, mainly square (based on a module of nine meters by nine meters) with their openings generally on the axes, seek solemnity in regularity. In their stateliness, they evoke something of the nineteenth-century galleries devoted to antiquities.

The elements that serve to break up, equalize, and redistribute the light (indispensable to the contemporary preference for natural light) are stationary. There is no recourse to complex devices that one day or another stop working. The cross-shaped plaster blades serve not only as deflectors but also as architectural signs; in their forceful neutrality and abstraction, they provide an equivalent to the painted ceilings in the Charles X galleries. Pei wanted his galleries to have a personality. The choice of relatively strong colors distinguishes them from the neighboring rooms. these are no longer the pale tones that have gained favor in the twentieth century but sharp greens and purples that, following the intuition of the nineteenth century, bring out the colors of the paintings all the more forcefully. Small rooms, associated with the idea of the intimacy and tiny formats of Northern painting, have not been forgotten; they line the central galleries along one side. These square, medium-size galleries, meanwhile are themselves conceived like more intimate exhibition spaces. Now rendered adequately vast, airy, and solemn, they recall that the Northern schools, far from being limited to modest formats and modest subjects, belong to the tradition of great painting.   Bruno Foucart 82

actors and its profound unity. With just a few exceptions, justified by the restoration of a historical group such as the great Medici Gallery or the existence of a de facto group as prestigious as that of the Rembrandts, this is a vision that excludes any "star system."

The visit begins in the direction of the Rue de Rivoli with the fifteenth-century Dutch and Flemish painters—Van Eyck, Bosch *(The Ship of Fools),* Memling—and leads to a large square gallery devoted to late fifteenth-century Germany. At that point, a long, stately chain of galleries extends from east to west with a series of more intimate little rooms bordering it on the Rue de Rivoli side. Along this linear path that is nonetheless festooned with little detours are arrayed in succession the Cranachs, Dürer, and Wolf Huber, the early sixteenth-century Flemish and Dutch painters (Joos van Cleve's *Descent from the Cross,* Quentin Metsys's *Banker and His Wife),* the Antwerp Mannerists, and Pieter

83

Brueghel the Elder's *Beggars).* Here, a small room for temporary exhibitions guarantees a graphic arts presence in the midst of this ocean of painting.

After a second half of the sixteenth century, with Jan "Velvet" Brueghel and Cornelis van Haarlem, comes the forceful north-south axis of the Rubens cycle. Between two high-ceilinged rooms containing very large-format religious subjects by Rubens, as well as Jacob Jordaens and van Thulden, a custom-renovated gallery (see page 64) provides the setting for the epic *Life of Marie de Médicis.* The logic of the times calls for crossing back through this gallery of royal vanities to the Rue de Rivoli side in order to arrive at the "small" Rubens (Helena Fourment and her children, various sketches), meet Van Dyck's *Charles I,* pass through seventeenth-century Flanders, and rub shoulders with the Northern Caravaggists (Gerrit van 84

see page 69

THE NEW MEDICI GALLERY

By Bruno Foucart, professor at the University of Paris IV (La Sorbonne).

The transfer of the Medici Gallery to the Richelieu wing is a major element in the transformation of the Grand Louvre. In order to understand why the reinstallation of these twenty-four large-format paintings was one of the most delicate problems to be resolved, suffice it to recall that the cycle depicting the life of Marie de Médicis is the largest, both physically and metaphysically, of those executed by the greatest of the Flemish painters, and that this cycle is to the Louvre what the Stanze della Signatura is to the Vatican. The fact of placing the Medici Gallery in the very center of the Richelieu wing, of installing it as the focus of all the Northern painting rooms, of trying to integrate its early and modern history into the presentation, reflects a desire to bring out its multiple roles: as the masterpiece of a painter, as a masterpiece of the Louvre, as a place of meditation, inspiration, and pictorial references.

This is in fact the fifth site and the sixth installation that the Medici Gallery has known. The cycle, devoted to the exceptional life of Marie de Médicis, wife of Henri IV, mother of Louis XII, and queen regent after her husband's assassination, was commissioned from Rubens by its subject in 1622 and inaugurated in 1625. It had been conceived for the west gallery of the Luxembourg Palace, along the front courtyard. It was to have been accompanied by a parallel cycle devoted to Henri in the east wing, but this was never completed. The paintings glorifying Marie de Médicis were transferred to this east wing, now a library, at the very beginning of the nineteenth century, when the Luxembourg Palace was given to the Senate and architect Jean-François Chalgrin stripped the interior of the gallery in order to install his monumental staircase. In 1815 the paintings were sent to the Louvre, a confirmation of their new status as exemplars of painterly genius. They were hung at random in the Grande Galerie until 1900, when they were reassembled in the third Hall of States, which had been left unfinished since the fall of the Second Empire. Gaston Redon, the brother of Odilon, conceived a neo-Rubensian decor, in gold and red, which was replaced in 1953 by the red and black schema of Moreux and Haffner.

The real historical concern has been to reconstitute the original arrangement as faithfully as possible. The twenty-four-painting ensemble was read from left to right. There were ten canvases on each of the long sides of the rectangular room. The portraits of the queen and her parents, Francesco de' Medici and Joanna of Austria, were placed at the entrance to the gallery opposite the *Apotheosis of Henri IV* that occupied the entire wall on the other end of the rectangle. In the Grande Galerie the paintings had lost their order and no longer benefited from a unified, closed space. Redon's arrangement in 1900 included only eighteen paintings; *The Council of the Gods for the Spanish Weddings* and two other parts of the series, as well as the portraits, had been placed outside, in the Van Dyck room. The three large canvases showing the *Coronation,* the *Apotheosis,* and the *Council of the Gods* no longer occupied the end of the gallery like the choir decorations of a church. The 1953 renovations allowed the narrative continuity to be reestablished, but the first and last paintings of the series had to be placed outside the gallery. The three portraits were still missing and had even been transferred to Versailles. Instead of eighteen paintings, there were now nineteen. In the Richelieu wing, they are finally back to twenty-four: for the first time in more than two hundred years, the three portraits watch over the epic historical unfolding of the episodes, which are themselves finally situated in their proper places in the queen regent's eventful life.

The other problem was that of defining the space. The original gallery, built in the French manner with a flat ceiling rather than a curved one, was a long, primitively narrow corridor measuring 58 x 7.5 meters. The canvases, inserted in moldings that are known only from a few documentary sources, were separated by lateral windows that provided them with natural light. This lighting had been criticized very early on, and after 85

85. In this image, one corner of the spectacular Medici Gallery is visible. The high, curved ceiling and 524 square meters of floor space permit the display of 24 monumental works related to the life of Marie de Médicis (1573-1642).

64

1799, when the paintings were transferred to the facing room, known as the Henri IV Gallery. Chalgrin responded to the new demand by introducing lunettes to create nearly overhead lighting. In the Louvre's Grande Galerie, in the Hall of States, and again in the Richelieu wing, the Marie de Médicis cycle enjoys this overhead lighting that, since Hubert Robert, has been synonymous with the palace-museum.

The dimensions of the new gallery essentially correspond to those of the old one. As it was refurbished by Redon or Haffner and Moreux, the Hall of States, forty meters long by fourteen meters wide, combined the advantages of gallery and salon. However imperfectly, it permitted the cycle to be presented in its chronological order and at the same time, seen in its totality from a central area and by a large public. Twice as wide as the original gallery, the Hall of States had accompanied, and even brought about, the changing nature of the Medici Gallery. Instead of a palatial decor limited to an intimate circle, it had in fact become a public lesson in total painting, the place where the hymns of Baroque color and expressiveness rang out most jubilantly.

By keeping the same general proportions and also giving the new room a barrel vault with overhead lighting, like that of the Grande Galerie, I. M. Pei has created the visual and spatial synthesis of gallery and great hall that defines the setting necessary for the presentation of these canvases. Inserted between the two blocks formed by the Richelieu pavilions and the library, the new gallery is nonetheless slightly more compact; indeed, it measures 39.5 x 13.26 meters, which limits the space available between the canvases. This was the main difficulty of the site. Redon, Haffner, and Moreux had conceived wide, triumphal frames, all gold and neo-Louis XIV for the first, all black and neo-Louis XIII for the second. I. M. Pei has defined the problem differently: to retrieve the spirit of the paintings enclosed, as in the Luxembourg Palace, in fairly low moldings and to create an architectural structure strong enough to keep the canvases quite separate while still allowing the eye to glide easily from one to the other. The pilasters bearing the ribs of the vault not only punctuate the gallery but define minimalist niches that serve as frames. The simplified profiles of the

molding and the lacquered surface tone down the projections and unify the vision.

Like Redon, the turn-of-the-century ecclectic, and Moreux and Haffner with their 1950s theatricality, Pei has opted for the spirit of his time, that of fin-de-siècle modernity: without any direct references, there is an acknowledgment of early and modern history, a decoration that is both present and absent. The black wood edging alludes

to the original frames from the time of Marie de Médicis, while the flat border in dark green and the smooth matte coating of the pilasters in pale green lacquer constitute a surrounding sufficiently neutral and complementary to accompany the Rubensian splendor with elegance. The gilt and the red have been excluded in favor of the complementary hue, namely green. A calm, forceful architecture-as-frame and a color scheme that accompanies and complements the brilliance of the Marie de Médicis cycle provide the essential elements of the creative new gallery installation.   B. F.

86. Portrait of Marie de Médicis, *by Peter Paul Rubens (o/c, 276 x 144 cm).*

87. *In this rather dense hanging of Flemish paintings, works by Roelant Savery and Valckenborch are visible. The color of the walls was chosen to bring out the paintings as much as possible.*

86

88. *Painting in seventeenth-century Amsterdam. From left to right, works by Jan Van der Heyden (*The Dam and the New Amsterdam City Hall*), Pieter de Hooch (*The Drinker, The Card Players *and *The Courtyard of a Dutch House*), and Jacob van Ruisdael's *Ray of Sunlight.

89. *This *Lace-Maker *(o/c, 24 × 21 cm, c. 1679) is one of two works by Vermeer in the Louvre. It was purchased by the museum in 1870 when this Dutch master was just beginning to be rediscovered.*

continued from page 62

Honthorst, Matthias Stomer). A small corridor overlooking the Marly courtyard leads to four galleries extending toward the Cour Napoléon. There we encounter the seventeenth-century Dutch painters and above all, the shock of an entire gallery virtually papered with Rembrandts: *The Slaughtered Ox, The Philosopher, Bathsheba,* and the self-portraits, but also, without a real hierarchy in the installation, the "afters" and "close tos" (Lastman) that place the singularity of Rembrandt's genius in context: the genius is evident, but not as isolated as the idolators would have it. This could be taken as one form of response to the somewhat brutal radicalism of the current revision of Rembrandt's corpus. The next gallery brings together "Rembrandt-like" painters such as Flinck, Victors, or Drost. The section ends with the second half of the seventeenth century, the genre

89

scenes of Adriaen van Ostade, the Gerard Dous, landscapes, still lifes and portraits by Jan Steen, Paulus Potter, and Gabriel Metsu, Jacob van Ruisdael's *Ray of Sunlight,* and finally the Vermeers (*The Lacemaker, The Astronomer*), so discreetly silent that it is almost too bad, after such a circuit, that their magnificent inlaid frames set them apart a bit from their neighbors.

From Charlemagne to Napoleon III

Just below the paintings, the Decorative Arts department occupies the entire first floor of the Richelieu wing. The Charlemagne gallery, the Scepter gallery, the Faenza corridor, the Thousand Flowers gallery, the Louis XII gallery, the Medals gallery, the Scipio gallery, the Adolphe de Rothschild gallery, the Holy Spirit gallery, the Effiat gallery: the Department of Decorative Arts draws on the history of humanity and that of the arts, on kings and donors, on

88

techniques and subjects, to call the roll, with a certain museological poetry, of the forty galleries that the expansion has offered it.

This is a royal gift for a comparable collection: 15,000 objects, of which 6,500 were presented in 1991 and 8,000 today, including 5,500 in the Richelieu wing alone. From this vast treasure, only a few items can be singled out as markers on the long path that begins at the great escalator and leads, not without a few detours, from the Middle Ages (now increased from two to eleven galleries) to the seventeenth century, then skips over the eighteenth century already in place around the Cour Carrée to pass through the (First) Empire and meet up with the Napoléon III apartments that are ready and waiting at right angles to the Turgot pavilion.

The treasures of the Abbey of St. Denis, the ceramics of Faenza, the enamels of Léonard Limosin, the great ceiling from the end of the Italian Renaissance reinstalled in the Adolphe de Rothschild gallery (named after its donor), the Renaissance bronzes from the collection of Louis XIV, the silver gilt objects of the Order of the Holy Spirit (displayed as if they were in a chapel, with retable, altar cloth, hangings, and embroidered knights' cloaks on mannequins), the Louis XIII bed, chairs, and cabinet from the château of Effiat, Anne of Austria's precious casket, and the empress Joséphine's jewel cabinet are only a few examples of this accumulation—carefully ordered, to be sure—of furniture, dishes, religious metalwork, curiosities, ceramics, stained-glass windows, bronzes, ivories, jewels, and tapestries. These last deserve special mention, for the monumental galleries devoted to *The History of Scipio* and *Maximilian's Hunts* (see page 72), which in themselves justify a visit to the Richelieu wing. Also worthy of attention, apart from the majesty of the spaces, is the play of the strong, refined colors of the walls: the green-ochre behind *Maximilian's Hunts,* the red for the *Scipio* series, which is nearly the complement of the preceding green, the reddish brown of the gallery devoted to the bronzes, or the deep greens and blues that change with the north-south light coming from the tall windows on the Rue de Rivoli side. Jean-Michel Wilmotte, the designer of these elegant galleries, has made his transition to color with them. In front of these muted, matte hues applied on projected plaster, the objects and their own tonalities take on their full value. And it should also be noted that in these chains of differently colored galleries, the hues harmonize without ever being placed side by side: the perfectly white treatment of the doorways, carried over to the window frames, creates strong vertical accents that impose a quasi-musical rhythm on the whole. Artificial lighting over these doors and windows maintains the effect when the natural light starts to fade. Even if these galleries were empty, they could be visited with pleasure.

All of France in Stone

Continuing the descent on the great escalator, one can go from Decorative Arts to the Department of Sculpture. On both sides of the Passage Richelieu leading from the Place du Palais-Royal to the Pyramid entrance, the Marly and

90. 91. 92. A Descent from the Cross *in ivory (Paris, third quarter of the thirteenth century);* an enamel Portrait of the Virgin in Prayer *by the Master of the Triptych of Louis XIII (Limoges, beginning of the sixteenth century) and an enameled reliquary representing the martyrdom of St. Thomas à Beckett (Limoges, thirteenth century). Three examples of the wealth of the Decorative Arts department of the Louvre.*

91

92

see page 79

90

71

MAXIMILIAN'S HUNTS

By Daniel Alcouffe, head curator, Department of Decorative Arts.

In their new quarters, the medieval and Renaissance collections of the Decorative Arts department will now occupy most of the first floor of the former Ministry of Finance. The considerable wall space thus acquired will undoubtedly attract more attention to the earliest tapestries in the department's collection, whose importance was perhaps overlooked in the past because of their unfortunate presentation over the display cases of the Colonnade galleries. This group of works provides a rather good overview of the evolution of tapestry weaving in western Europe between the fifteenth and early seventeenth centuries. Among the fifteenth-century examples are works attributed to Arras and Tournai. Brussels's Golden Age is represented by the tapestries that were, from 1476 on, inevitably designed by painters. There are also the *millefleurs* ("thousand flowers") whose production was claimed by both France and Flanders, Italian tapestries from Ferrara and Florence, English tapestries from the Mortlake workshop, founded in 1619, and French tapestries, reflecting the art of the School of Fontainebleau and later on, products of the Louvre and other Parisian workshops of the Louis XIII era.

The collection has been built up through every form of acquisition. Certain tapestries were purchased, such as those that came—quite early on—from the collection of the Troubadour painter Pierre Révoil, acquired in 1828. Others were donated, like the Brussels-woven *Last Judgment,* which was the Friends of the Louvre Society's first gift to the department, in 1901, or the three *millefleurs* with pastoral subjects from the Larcade donation. In 1991, the dation in payment (a form of estate settlement) brought the Louvre two other *millefleurs*

from the collection of Martin Le Roy. Still other tapestries come from the former Crown collections, including the eight pieces of the Gobelins *History of Scipio.* And finally, in the same category, is *Maximilian's Hunts,* one of the great masterpieces in the Louvre. The twelve pieces of this set had in fact been reunited since 1938, when they were given an appropriately large room in the northern half of the Colonnade wing, but they were hung too high to be properly appreciated.

It is quite remarkable that so many separate pieces, the largest of which is 7.5 meters long, were never divided up in

the course of their history, and that this set was saved from the destruction of the Crown tapestries ordered by the Directory in order to retrieve the gold and silver thread. Clearly, its beauty has always inspired respect.

Woven in Brussels around 1530 from cartoons that were probably designed by the painter Bernard van Orley, a favorite at the Flemish court, the set illustrates the twelve months of the year with a series of hunting scenes that take place in the Soignes forest southwest of Brussels. The first tapestries, *March* to *June,* show the preparations for the hunt; *July* to *October,* the stag hunt;

93. The Adolphe de Rothschild room presents religious metalwork from the Middle Ages to the Renaissance, given by the Baron at the beginning of the century. The ceiling, from a 16th century Venetian palace was also purchased through his generosity.

94. One of the largest spaces in the Louvre, the gallery designed for the 12 tapestries of the series of Maximilian's Hunts, woven in Brussels between 1531 and 1533, probably on the basis of cartoons by the painter Bernard van Orley.

Following double page:
95. Eight of the Gobelins tapestries representing the History of Scipio *are displayed in a large room that is perpendicular to the Maximilian Gallery.*

November to January, the boar hunt. *February* brings the cycle to a close with an homage to King Modus and Queen Ratio, protagonists of a fourteenth-century hunting treatise.

In magnificent landscapes of forests and ponds, the various episodes present a multitude of characters whose lively poses are rendered with remarkable exactness. Certain figures with particularly defined features have been the subject of numerous attempts to identify them with different members of the Habsburg family, all of whom were great hunters: the emperor Maximilian—erroneously, although the set has borne his name since the seventeenth century—and with greater likelihood, his grandchildren.

The set provides a unique document of court life, in which the hunt occupied such an important position, and more specifically, of life at the Brussels court in the sixteenth century. It depicts certain royal residences in minute detail: the ducal palace in Brussels with its park (*March* and *February*) and the Château of Tervueren (*January*), as well as the imperial hunt in Boitsfort (*April*). It chronicles the luxury of men's and women's costumes of the era and even the wealth of the imperial metalwork.

Counterpointing the princely hunt, the daily life of those who do not participate is hardly forgotten: young horsemen practice in the park of the Brussels château (*March*); the monks of the Priory of Rouge-Cloître go for a stroll (*July*); skaters glide around the Château of Tervueren (*January*); the Courtyard of the Buckets in the ducal palace is full of onlookers (*February*); a couple of lovers wander off by themselves (*May*). This narrative, where scenes of cruelty have been excluded, where the brutality of the sport is tempered by the presence of many women, gives off a joie de vivre that transforms it into a hymn to youth.

Strangely enough, the person who commissioned the set still remains unknown, but this is not the case for the great collectors who were subsequently to have the honor of possessing it: the dukes of Guise, Cardinal Mazarin, Louis XIV. The Gobelins workshop was to copy it many times in the seventeenth and eighteenth centuries, and the *Hunts* of Louis XV were to provide an updated version in the typically precious style of the eighteenth century.   D. A.

96. 97. 98. 99. A gold casket named after Anne of Austria (Paris, seventeenth century); a large Hispano-Moorish plate with the arms of Moncade (fifteenth century); a detail of an elaborate table decoration in marble and gilded bronze by Valadier (eighteenth century, detail). To the right, an agate cup representing a lion, which is displayed in the Apollo gallery of the Cour Carrée (Sarachi atelier, Milan, end of the sixteenth century).

continued from page 71

Puget courtyards with their elegant skylights will undoubtedly become "musts" for the tour of the Louvre, for it is around them that the French sculpture section is organized on the ground floor of the museum.

The geography of the galleries had to take into account

100. *The* Courajod Christ *is named after the donor who gave the work in 1895. It is one of first masterpieces of French sculpture displayed around the Marly and Puget-courtyards (polychromed wood, h. 157 cm high, Burgundy, second quarter of the twelfth century).*

101. *This* Virgin of Sorrows *is a polychromed terra cotta model (h. 178 cm, c. 1585) for a marble sculpture that was to be placed in the uncompleted Valois rotunda at the Abbey of St. Denis.*

101

spaces that were often already quite well defined or supporting walls that could obviously not be shifted. And it is useless to dwell on the difficulty of installing such a department when it was necessary to move more than a thousand sculptures, often quite heavy and/or fragile, over long distances. Many of them have just been brought out of the storerooms (which remain heavily stocked nonetheless). The ordering of the section is simple and can be divided up in large blocks of space and colors. The Middle Ages occupies the galleries along the south; on the west is the Marly courtyard, with its walls covered in pale stucco; the Renaissance and the seventeenth century are along the Rue de Rivoli, against burnt-sienna walls; the eighteenth century, on a gray-green that brings out the whiteness of the marbles without competing with the often strong colors of the original bases that have been preserved (the new ones are

see page 82

100

THE MARLY COURTYARD

With the coming of the Grand Louvre, the Department of Sculpture, formerly quartered in the remote Flore wing, has finally received the space it warrants on the ground floor of the Richelieu wing. French seventeenth-century sculpture in particular will now occupy the Marly and Puget courtyards on either side of the Passage Richelieu.

The first of these, the Marly courtyard, is one of the most successful of the newly remodeled spaces. It takes its name from the sculptures displayed there, masterpieces of French art from the reign of Louis XIV that once decorated the gardens of the Marly château. The Sun King had sought such a property so that he might (without going too far from Versailles) "enjoy a bit of rest from time to time and be by himself with a few of his special favorites from the court." After acquiring the estate in 1676, he had a small château and twelve pavilions built between 1679 and 1686 by Jules Hardouin-Mansart, the architect of the Gallery of the Mirrors at Versailles and the golden dome of the Invalides in Paris.

The garden and the building were conceived as a vast, harmonious ensemble on the Italian model, with "nature" structured just as much as the château. The whole formed a sumptuous setting charged with a mix of symbolism from antique and royal mythology intended to glorify the ruler, who was identified with the sun. As at Versailles, water played a preponderant role, with an abundance of waterfalls, ponds, and fountains. All that remained was to provide the estate with the necessary sculptures. The first to be installed were antique copies (stored at Versailles) cast by the Kellers or sculpted in marble by artists such as Pierre Le Pautre (the *Faun with a Kid,* 1685) or François Barois (*Venus Callipygos,* 1683). Since the general theme of the program was given, the artists had only to plunge into antique mythology, especially the eclogues and pastorales. Anselme Flamen's *Diana,* for example, was subsequently to be surrounded by the goddess's "companions."

The first major commission was given to Antoine Coysevox in 1698; over the next four years he was to complete the two groups of *The King's Fame* for the Abreuvoir (horse-pond) and four others for La Rivière: *The Seine, The Marne,*

Neptune, and *Amphitrite.* With the figure of the water god Neptune, Coysevox reoriented the rigor of Classicism; the movement with which he invested the divinity prefigured the Rocaille style that was to prevail several years later. This same ardor reappears in the *Fame* and *Mercury* mounted on winged horses representing Pegasus and proclaiming the glory of the monarch. For these two groups Coysevox obtained the largest stipend ever allocated to an artist by Louis XIV, who was extremely satisfied with the results. Several years later, in 1708, the sculptor was to receive a new commission for a *Pan,* a *Hamadryad (Nymph of the Woods),* and a *Flora* intended as a group for the Green Apartments, where they were paired up with another group by Nicolas Coustou composed of an *Adonis* or *Hunter at Rest* and *Two Nymphs* (1710).

Also solicited by the sovereign for the decoration of the ponds around the château were Le Pautre (*Atalante,* 1703-1705), Nicolas Coustou (*Apollo,* 1713-1714), and his brother Guillaume (*Daphne,* 1713-1714). Nicolas Coustou's *The Seine and the Marne* and Corneille van Clève's *The Loire and the Loiret,* traditional figures of rivers that decorate the ornamental Bassin de Nappes, were completed around 1700-1705.

Louis XIV's death in 1715 did not prevent the continuation of the sculpture commissions. Although Marly was to remain uninhabited during the Regency, several works were still installed in the park, sometimes just before their transfer to the Tuileries. This was the case with the two groups by Le Pautre, *Arria and Poetus,* created in Rome during the 1690s and brought to Marly in 1715, and *Aeneas and Anchises,* completed in 1716.

It was not until 1745, however, that the famed horses of Guillaume Coustou replaced those of Coysevox, which had been transferred to the Tuileries gardens several years earlier. Nephew and former pupil of Coysevox, Coustou was to create for Marly the masterpiece that subsequently brought him his fame, and this in barely two years, at least for the cutting of the marble. Escaping all traditional iconography, the celebrated *Horses of Marly* are a totally original creation, without direct reference to

102. The Marly courtyard evokes the former splendor of the Château of Marly through the presence of the main sculptures that once decorated its gardens, including the celebrated Horses of Marly by Guillaume Coustou.

antique mythology or any ideological or political repertory. The horses held back by grooms—one symbolizing America, the other Europe—express quite simply the savage strength of the animal that man attempts to restrain. With an astonishing technical mastery, they evoke the baroque ardor and expressive vigor of Guillaume Coustou, who is quite different in that respect from his brother Nicolas, more dependent on the lessons of classical antiquity. Brought to the entrance of the Champs-Élysées in 1794, the *Horses of Marly* were deposited in the Louvre in 1984 because of the threat of pollution. Replicas have since been placed on the Champs-Elysées.

All of these sculptures from Marly have thus been brought together in the courtyard, which occupies the former site of the Ministry of Finance parking lot. Here, they benefit from natural light through the courtyard's transparent covering, as well as a space sufficently large to suggest their original placement. Without going so far as to reconstitute their respective positions in the park of Marly (which would be impossible), the curators have chosen a presentation that privileges the understanding of the works in relation to one another.

The installation of the courtyard nonetheless encountered significant difficulties, since the opening of the Passage Richelieu broke the continuity of the visit on the ground-floor level within the Department of Sculpture itself. In order to reestablish this continuity, it became necessary to dig an underground passage (see interview). This makes it possible to go directly from the Puget courtyard to the Marly courtyard without interrupting the seventeenth-century French sculpture circuit.

But the main innovation of this installation lies in the transparency that characterizes these courtyards. In addition to the skylights that allow the penetration of natural light, the side openings into the Passage Richelieu have been preserved, thus permitting visitors to look outside but also allowing pedestrians taking the Passage Richelieu to see the interior of the courtyards and the works they can contain. This is probably the first time that a museum is offering this kind of opening to the outside world, and it is a radically new concept: transparency as a direct invitation to enter the museum.   Sylvie Blin

continued from page 79

made of the same rose-colored stone from Burgundy that covers the floors), and the nineteenth century is similarly displayed in the last galleries of the section, extended by a terrace along the Puget courtyard.

Entering through the Marly courtyard, the visit begins with the late Middle Ages and the great Romanesque sculpture of Auvergne, Burgundy, and Languedoc (including the celebrated *Courajod Christ* in a wall recess). The Gothic is

103

next with the tall column-statues from Corbeil, *Solomon and the Queen of Sheba* (c. 1160-1180), elements from Chartres, Reims, and Bourges, then a series of images of Mary around the magnificent *Blanchelande Virgin.* These are followed by various tomb sculptures in a crypt-like setting and then a group of fifteenth-century works (from Burgundy, Ile-de-France, Berry, Auvergne, and Lorraine) around the impressive funerary monument of Philippe Pot, with his prostrate body carried by eight hooded official mourners. Michel Colomb, the moving tomb of Renée d'Orléans, the chapel of the Commynes evoked by its praying and prostrate figures and various architectural elements brought out of storage make the transition from fifteenth to sixteenth centuries, notably with pieces from the Troie school at the northwest corner of the Marly courtyard. Next to a window, and thus quite visible from the

104

arcades of the Rue de Rivoli like an honored guest at the museum, is *Diana the Huntress;* with Jean Goujon, Michel Anguier, and others, the great French Renaissance is upon us. And it is a natural step to enter the spectacular Marly courtyard set up around Guillaume Coustou's celebrated *Horses of Marly* and the great allegories of Antoine Coysevox (see page 80).

Stairways lead under the Passage Richelieu toward the Puget courtyard, structured with a series of terraces housing the reliefs and medallions of the Place des Victoires around the group of *Captives* and the great *Milon of Croton.*

Four tall potted fig trees toward the far end of the courtyard soften somewhat the severity of this mineral world.

105

Preceding double page:
103. *In the sculpture galleries, looking towards the Rue de Rivoli, this room includes several works by Pradier, including his* Three Graces. In *the center, Dumont's* Genius of Liberty *best known through the cast which is at the center of the Bastille square.*

104. *This* Diana the Huntress *by Jean Goujon (c. 1550) was made at the same time that the sculptor began his work at the Louvre. It was intended for the castle of Diane de Poitiers at Anet and is exhibited today in the Renaissance sculpture rooms along the Rue de Rivoli.*

105. *The selection of French sculpture in the Richelieu wing ranges from the early Romanesque to the nineteenth century, with works such as this* Orlando Furioso *by Jehan Du Seigneur (bronze, 1867, detail), placed on a terrace overlooking the Puget courtyard.*

106. *A work by Pierre Puget, whose name was given to one of the courtyards in the Richelieu wing (*Hercules at Rest, *marble, h. 160 cm, 1661-1662).*

A side staircase leads back up to the eighteenth-century galleries, which are placed like a series of alcoves around a central corridor lined with statues reminiscent of the former gallery of great men. Thus Poussin, Corneille, Racine, Voltaire, and Montesquieu, among other illustrious personalities, lead the visitor to the works of Jean Houdon, Etienne Falconet, Michel Clodion, Jean-Jacques Caffieri, Jean-Baptiste Pigalle, and Augustin Pajou. One of these alcoves brings together nearly the entire collection—until now largely kept in storage—of the presentation pieces for entry into the Academy, one of the many rediscoveries made possible by the renovation. The section ends with the time of the Revolution and the Empire and, spilling onto the U-shaped terrace that surrounds the Puget courtyard, the sculptors of the Romantic movement such as Du Seigneur, James Pradier, François Rude, and Antoine-Louis Barye.

106

The Millennial East

Adjoining the sculptures on the ground floor, the Department of Oriental Antiquities surrounds the Khorsabad courtyard, which, with its rather theatrical presentation, creates a new focus of public attention within this enormous Louvre (see page 88). Sumer, Mari, Babylon, Nineveh, and Byblos are names that mark the dawn of civilization, the birth of the city and that of writing and laws, of enormous palaces abandoned to the desert and gradually recovered, and gigantic archives engraved in clay and miraculously preserved until their recent rediscovery. A vast Oriental dream linked to reality by fabulous bas-reliefs and gigantic capitals, enigmatic statues of governors and princes, protected in its mystery by apparently unwavering colossi like the "being whose lion's breast, joined to a bull's body and equipped with eagle's wings, is crowned with a human head, this marvel of creation and oasis of thought," that André Parrot described in speaking of the figures coming from Khorsabad, which he compared to the tetramorph surrounding the figure of Christ on the tympana of Romanesque churches.

Some five thousand pieces, from the most monumental to the smallest—and that was just one among many problems of installing this department—are thus reintegrated into a more spacious presentation that permits each object to be better appreciated. Whether objects of art or objects of daily use, precious or modest, monumental or fragmentary, each one is bathed in the aura that surrounds rare witnesses of civilizations that have disappeared for millennia, and all enjoy equal attention in their presentation. The light is usually natural, with walls of beige stucco, display cases with gray frames and light-colored fittings. The first gallery immediately carries the visitor back to the third millennium B.C. with Sumer, Tello, and Mari, the renowned city-states of ancient Mesopotamia. There, *Ebih-Il, the Governor of Mari,* sculpted in alabaster, still awaits the orders of his king, and a wall screen bears the famous *Stele of the Vultures* from Lagash. At right angles, a long gallery offers the visual shock of a row of likenesses of Gudea, prince of Lagash. Another gallery along the north side of the Khorsabad courtyard evokes the palace of Mari and the quasi-mythic Babylon with the 2.25 meters of dressed basalt bearing the code of Hammurabi (eighteenth-seventeenth centuries B.C.), the forerunner of all our legal texts. At the other end of this gallery, the rear wall is faced with bricks from the Ishtar Gate (the great "Passing Lion" of the sixth century). Toward the south, a long gallery with alcoves along the

see page 92

107. This small figure (h. 11,7 cm), acquired in 1961, is from Bactria (Afghanistan). It is one of the most exceptional objects in the Oriental Antiquities department.

107

108. This fragmentary object is known as the Stele of the Vultures *(Tello, c. 2450 B.C.). Not on display for a number of years, it is one of the earliest known representations of an historic battle between the kings of Lagash and Umma.*

108

THE KHORSABAD COURTYARD

By Annie Caubet, head curator, Department of Oriental Antiquities.

It was exactly 150 years ago, in the spring of 1843, that the French consul in Mosul, Paul-Emile Botta, first began excavating the mounds of ruins over which the modern-day village of Khorsabad had risen. The appearance of great stone reliefs led to the rediscovery not of Nineveh as Botta believed, but of a new capital built in the late eighth century B.C. by King Sargon II and bearing his name (Dur Sharrukin, or "Sargon's fortress"). This was, at the same time, the first discovery of Assyrian civilization.

Botta continued the excavation in 1844 with the help of painter Eugène Flandin, whose precise drawings permitted the organization of the palace decorations to be understood. The gateways were framed with a monumental composition including winged bulls (*lamassu*) and huge mythological figures, either winged genies or lion-conquering heros identified with Gilgamesh. In the rooms inside, the bases of the walls were lined with a frieze of stone slabs (orthostats) applied to the brick masonry.

A first selection of sculptures arrived in Paris after making their way down the Tigris on goatskin-lined rafts. In 1847, the Louvre's curator of antiquities, Adrien de Longpérier, was thus able to open the first "Assyrian Museum" in Europe. Its pink marble plaque is still visible over a doorway in the northeast corner of the Cour Carrée.

Botta had chosen to send two winged bulls from the throne room to the Louvre, but in order to haul them from the site at Khorsabad to the Tigris, sixteen kilometers away, he had to have them cut up, into five and six pieces, respectively. Victor Place, who succeeded Botta in 1852-1853, was better equipped and managed to send a whole group of large reliefs intact. Unfortunately, part of his convoy fell prey to looters not far from Basra, and only one *lamassu* survived the attack. Even with this disaster, Place's shipments necessitated an enlargement of the Assyrian Museum. The collections were transferred to a nearby gallery, designed by the Neoclassical architect Fontaine and arranged for the Assyrian antiquities by Hector-Martin Lefuel, one of the architects of the Musée Napoléon III that was inaugurated in 1857.

A fourth bull was executed in plaster to serve as a pendant to the one received from Place, and the two pairs of *lamassu* were installed at right angles to their original position. The genies were separated from the bulls and placed in high wall niches alternating with the orthostats from the continuous friezes. Such a presentation, while hardly faithful to the letter of Assyrian architecture, at least respected its monumentality. These rooms, further enhanced with antiquities from other Assyrian capitals such as Nimrud and Nineveh, underwent no significant changes until 1991, and it was not without hesitation that the department decided to dismantle them.

The works formerly in the Cour Carrée will thus be reunited around what will now be called the Khorsabad courtyard, which has been specially redesigned by the architectural firm of Pei Cobb Freed, and notably Stephen Rustow, to accommodate the stone decorations of Sargon II's palace.

The height of the Khorsabad courtyard allows the winged bulls and mythological heros to be replaced in their original positions. A neutral vertical structure has been built within the space of the courtyard and a vaulted passageway inserted according to the measurements calculated from the third gateway of the town's fortifications (which was discovered intact by Place and recorded in photographs of the period). The passageway is framed by Botta's bulls and the winged genius that Place removed from this gateway. The foundations of the monumental reliefs have been sunken into the ground as they were in ancient times in order to guarantee their stability. Visitors will thus find themselves in the same position, relative to the height of the mythological creatures, as was the case in Assyrian times.

The facade of the throne room is freely evoked on the opposite wall. Two windows opening onto the Gudea room are framed by Place's bull and the nineteenth-century plaster replica; in the center, a cast of a bull turning its head toward the viewer, the original of which is located in the Oriental Institute in Chicago, is paired up with the most colossal of the Louvre's hero-and-lion sculptures, thus reconstituting a group that had been separated for 150 years.

109. *The Khorsabad Courtyard is meant to evoque the walls of the palace of Sargon II (8th century B.C.). The winged bulls visible here are no less than five meters high.*

109

The friezes, showing the *Transport of the Cedars of Lebanon, Bearers of the King's Furnishings,* and *Medean Tribute-Bearers,* have come down to us in an extremely fragmentary state. They were completed in the nineteenth century with plaster restorations executed from Eugène Flandin's drawings. The museum considers that the plaster additions, executed on the basis of highly accurate drawings made in situ at the time of the discovery, now have a documentary value that is practically equal to that of the drawings, and it was therefore decided to treat them as if they were originals and preserve them.

Once this choice was made, it was necessary to devise a means of dismantling the decoration (which had been reconstructed bit by bit in the walls of Napoléon III's ninetheenth-century Louvre) and to unify the different elements that today include the reliefs, ancient stone, modern plaster and brick, iron bolts, and so forth. This was accomplished by Michel Bourbon, who, with the help of Bovis Transport, created a system of metal frames that was used for the dismantling, transport, and reassembly in the new spaces.

The friezes are thus applied to the modern structure built within the Khorsabad courtyard. A corridor inside this structure will be accessible to specialists so that they can examine the inscriptions and masons' marks on the back of the reliefs. Rising five meters above the orthostats, this structure will give the public an idea of the original height of the mud-brick walls that had the stone reliefs applied to their bases. As with the bulls and the genies, the reliefs have been systematically reinstalled at their original height. In certain cases, such as the frieze of the *Medean Tribute-Bearers,* the surviving fragments are lower than the eye-level of an adult; in others, such as the *Dignitaries,* the heads will be nearly 3.5 meters above ground level.

This new installation is hardly intended to reproduce the exact layout of the ancient monument, for too many elements remain unknown. Rather, its aim is to allow the public to appreciate the real scale of this palatial architecture, the function of each relief in relation to the whole, and the symbolic significance of the wall decoration and the mythological creatures who guard the passages and who will be watching over the Khorsabad Courtyard from now on.   A. C.

110

111

112

110. *The* Fertility Goddess *decorating this fragment of an ivory pyxis cover from Ugarit (h. 13.5 cm, thirteenth century B.C.) shows clear links to the art of the Aegean.*

111. *The city-states of Cyprus were under Assyrian authority at the time of the Akkadian dynasty. This bowl decorated with chased and gilded silver dates from the end of the eighth or the beginning of the seventh century B.C. (d. 17.1 cm).*

112. *These gobelets and bowl, decorated with geometric motifs or stylized animal silhouettes (the tallest measures 28.9 cm) show the level of quality attained by the potters of Susa at the beginning of the fourth millennium B.C.*

113. *Gudea was the ruler of the Sumerian city-state of Lagash. The various images of him carved in black diorite figure among the masterpieces of world sculpture. This one is 70.5 cm high (c. 2150 B.C.).*

continued from page 86

Khorsabad courtyard brings the visitor to Anatolia and some rather little-known collections, then to Assyria, with the ultra-rare fragments of wall paintings found on the site of Til Barsip and also the little basalt bulls and the famous ivories of Arslan Tash. The cities of Nimrud and Nineveh come next. The ancient Iran section goes around the rotunda attached to the Cour Carrée, already bordered on the north by the Iran galleries. In this part are the Achemenids, with the huge, impressive bull protome capitals of the fifth or fourth century B.C. or the delicate and very well-known gold and silver ibex of the fourth century B.C.

For those who want to follow the chronology, a half-turn at the Marengo crypt leads back to the west side of the Cour Carrée, where the Department of Oriental Antiquities will now occupy half of the ground floor with the Near East up to the Iron Age: Cyprus, Syria (Byblos, Ugarit), and Palestine. Those who are willing to abandon the chronology a little can forego the half-turn at the door to the Marengo crypt in favor of the Persian and Greek sarcophagi and then, continuing in the north wing of the Cour Carrée, take in one last gallery evoking the splendor of Palmyra, Yemen and the caravan cities, and the hellenization of Syria and Cyprus. The leap into our era is made, and the mysteries of the ancient East are about to give way to Greco-Roman humanism. But that is another story, and another department of the Louvre, 114 outside the Richelieu wing.

Islam Recognized at Last

It is in the basement, and there are only thirteen galleries directly accessible from a stairway in Oriental Antiquities, but the Islamic Arts section—for this is not (as yet?) a separate department of the Louvre—is nonetheless the great beneficiary of the museum's expansion. These first-rate collections, numerous, abundant, varied, and as worthy of interest as they are largely ignored by the public because they have never yet been exhibited to their full extent, are finally getting their due. It was only time, given the task of evoking some thirteen centuries of art and civilization, spanning a cultural geography that, from the Bay of Bengal to the Atlantic, covers an area much larger than the one, for example, in which the flowering of the Renaissance or the Neoclassical revival took place.

In fact, North Africa is absent: it has its place in the Museum of African and Oceanic Arts (the former Museum of the Colonies) in Paris. These thirteen fairly low, vaulted galleries (they used to be cellars) form a rather labyrinthine sequence, which is not lacking in charm and goes along with certain features of Islamic architecture. In the absence of natural light, the multiplicity of materials and colors—the iridescence of glasses, the patina of bronze, the sparkle of gold and silver, the whiteness of marble and ivory, the shimmer of carpets, the reflections of ceramics, the mellow surface of wood—led to the choice of walls soberly coated with sand-colored stucco or painted in white, of the most neutral display cases possible, discreetly lined with fabrics of warm beige, pale yellow, soft green, or lavender blue. The indirect lighting, just as soft, is reinforced on the objects with the direct light of spots.

The proposed visit begins with the origins of Islam—and goes back even a bit farther to bring out certain relationships—then proceeds to display the splendors of the different great dynasties up to the Ottoman Empire. For those who are unfamiliar with this cultural and geographic 115

114. *This precious fragment of an Assyrian mural painting from the eighth century B.C. was found on the site of Til Barsip.*

115. 116. *The Oriental Antiquities section in the Richelieu wing now continues those already existing on the west and north of the Cour Carrée, notably the galleries devoted to ancient Iran. Seen here, a fragment of the famous* Frieze of the Archers of Darius *(enameled brick, late sixth-early fifth century B.C.) and a group of bronze horse bits (Luristan, eighth century B.C.).*

116

mosaic, the first gallery offers a large relief map of the "Islamic world" and a panel with the dynasties and explanatory texts. A side corridor decorated with carved wooden screens, which is in fact a blind passage unsuitable for presenting objects, offers a survey of Islamic architecture through plans and photos. In the galleries, the labels for the objects are well developed and others address wider themes, such as a site, a technique, or a typology.

Capitals from Susa, a milestone from the era of Caliph 'Abd al-Malik, and a large display case of glasswork fill the first gallery, devoted to the beginnings of Islam in the seventh century. Next comes the Abbassid period (750-1258), with cases devoted to typical decorative motifs (derived alternately from Greco-Roman and Sasanian traditions), others to ceramic innovations (metallic lustre, cobalt blue decoration, both inspired from China), and to woodwork. The third gallery presents two local dynasties of the classical period, the Umayyads of Spain and the Fatimids of Egypt, includ-

ing the extraordinary ivory pyxis carved for al-Mughira, the son of the Umayyad caliph 'Abd al-Rahman III. Next come three Iranian galleries, with the famous "Saint-Josse Shroud" from Khurasan, the no-less-famous *Plate of Knowledge*, the oldest-known celestial sphere (1147), and large displays of ceramics and scientific instruments. Still more ceramics, as well as objects of inlaid bronze and brass, are displayed in the small gallery allotted to the Seljuks of Iran (eleventh-thirteenth centuries). Then there is a gallery of funerary art filled with some twenty stelae, mostly from the first three centuries of Islam. The next gallery is quite diversified, with twelfth- and thirteenth-century works from Egypt, the Near East, and Anatolia side by side around the very famous "Baptistry of St. Louis," a masterpiece of Mamluk metalwork. Other Mamluk arts appear in a kind of rotunda with a large pillar: enameled glass mosque lamps, tapestries, metalwork. A corridor devoted to Mongol Iran leads to the galleries carved out under the Khorsabad courtyard and displaying the art of Timurid, Safavid, and Qajar Iran. Completely unexpected is a Western-style oil painting of the Qajar ruler Fath 'Ali Shah that was received as a gift by Napoléon I. The rugs in the collection, which are quite numerous but also fragile, will be exhibited in rotation so as to avoid too much exposure to the light.

This winding path finally reaches the Sublime Porte: the Ottoman world (fourteenth to twentieth century) displays the splendors of its ceramics, domestic or decorative and its jades inlaid with gold. The visit ends with a room reserved for the miniatures and calligraphies of India, Iran, Turkey, and the Arabian peninsula, also shown in rotation.   D. P.

117

ISLAMIC ART AT THE LOUVRE
By Marthe Bernus-Taylor, head curator, Islamic section.

The Louvre's Islamic art collections include about six thousand objects covering a geographical area that extends from Spain to India. With the exception of objects coming from the French excavations in Susa, (mostly fragments), these collections are the result of gifts, bequests, or purchases, and taken as a whole, they reflect the history of taste, and in particular the emergence of Orientalism, at the end of the nineteenth century. But it must also be recalled that several prestigious pieces belonged to royal collections. Among the objects from the cathedral treasury of St. Denis exhibited in the Apollo Gallery, for example, is a handsome rock-crystal ewer, an early eleventh-century work from Fatimid Egypt that was given to the abbey by the abbot Suger. The famous inlaid brass basin known as the "Baptistry of St. Louis," which is signed by the artist Muhammad ibn Zayn, a Syrian coppersmith active around the year 1300, is said to have been used for the baptism of Louis XIII. Formerly kept in the Sainte Chapelle of the Château of Vincennes and placed in the Louvre in 1852, it was brought to Notre-Dame Cathedral for the baptism of the imperial prince in 1856.

We do not know how the St. Denis ewer or the "Baptistry of St Louis" arrived in France. On the other hand, it would seem that the jade bowls inlaid with gold and precious stones that are listed in the inventories of Louis XIV came from the imperial Ottoman workshops of the Topkapi palace in the sixteenth century and were offered as diplomatic gifts. The large official portrait of Fath 'Ali Shah, the Qajar Iranian ruler, meanwhile, was sent to Napoléon I through the intermediary of his ambassador to Persia, A. Jaubert.

The "Muslim Arts Section" was created within the Department of Decorative Arts in 1890, following the Sauvageot donation and owing to the interest of two curators, Gaston Migeon and Emile Molinier. Migeon, who was to devote his life to the Louvre, was an eclectic collector who knew how to encourage gifts by

117, 118. From Spain to Turkey to India, Islamic art manifests a remarkable combination of unity and diversity. A Moghul miniature from the end of the sixteenth century shows Emperor Babur meeting with Badi'-al-Zaman Mirza (gouache, 24.5 × 23 cm). The Peacock Plate (underglaze painted ceramic, d. 37.5 cm, detail) is one of the masterpieces from the Iznik pottery workshops in the sixteenth century.

118

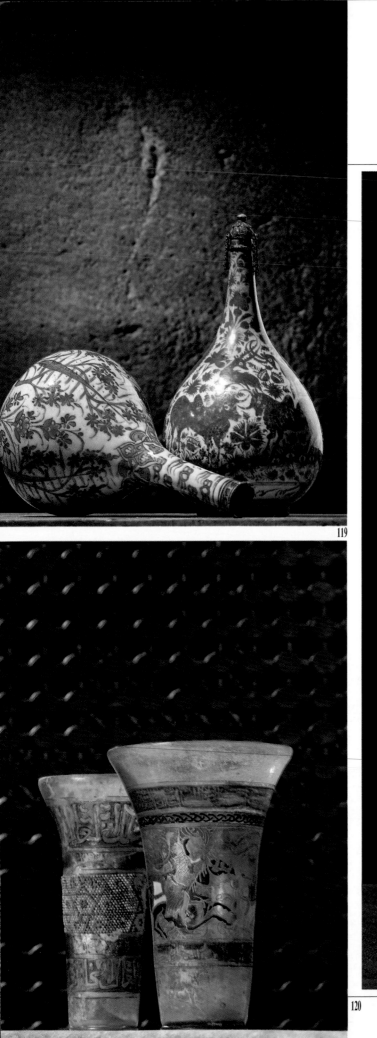

119

120

121

providing a good example himself. In 1905 he inaugurated a room devoted to Islamic arts, thus stimulating collectors to enrich it with further gifts.

Indeed, the same year saw Charles Piet Lataudrie donate thirteen works, including several major pieces of the Islamic collections. There are, for example, only two other known versions of the famous twelfth-century candlestick from Khurasan. Among the ceramics may be noted the very beautiful panel of cross- and star-shaped units in lustreware with blue highlights, every part of which is decorated with different vegetal, animal, or figurative motifs. Dated 1267, it comes from the tomb of the imam Ja'far in Damghan. Lataudrie's taste and eclecticism are perfectly apparent in the choice, among others, of four pieces of Ottoman ceramics characteristic of the changing production in Iznik between 1480 and 1570.

In 1912 another major expansion took place when the baronness Alphonse Delort de Gléon bequeathed the remarkable collection of some fifty objects acquired by her husband, a mining engineer and architect, in the Near East and Egypt. Every technique is represented. Among the metalwork, for example, is a ewer made in Damascus in 1258 by Husayn ibn Muhammad al-Mawsili for the Ayyubid sultan of Aleppo, al-Malik al-Nasir Salah al-Din Yusuf (the same ruler for whom the extraordinary vase that came to the Louvre from the collections of Pope Urban VIII was made). In addition to this bequest, the baroness left a large sum of money for the installation of a new and larger gallery, which, named after its donor, was inaugurated in 1922 on the second floor of the Clock pavilion (pavillon de l'Horloge).

From this period of Migeon's career date several other major gifts, including those of Georges Doisteau, Léon Dru, Joanny Benoît Peytel, the marquise Arconati-Visconti, Georges Marteau and Raymond Koechlin. Among the pieces Koechlin donated to the Louvre in 1893 and 1914 are several first-class works from Iran and Egypt or Sicily.

A new stage was marked by the Georges Marteau Bequest, which represents the most important contribution to date for the art of the book. Marteau, one of the great turn-of-the-century collectors of Oriental miniatures, followed the example set in the 1880s by Samuel Bing and Louis Gonse, who also launched the interest in things Japanese. The Universal Exposition of 1878 had already introduced the public to Middle Eastern art, which became the subject of a major fad at the time of the "Muslim Art" exhibits of 1893 and 1903. The second of these presented, along with the collections of Gonse (from which the Louvre recently acquired two miniatures) and Bing, those of figures who subsequently became famous in the field and bequeathed several masterpieces to the Louvre: Raymond Koechlin, Henri Vever, Léon Dru, Henri d'Allemagne, and Octave Homberg. It was indeed with Henri Vever that Georges Marteau prefaced and annotated the major publication devoted to "Persian" miniatures presented at the Museum of Decorative Arts in 1912. The eighty-three miniatures and calligraphies that Vever bequeathed illustrate the high points of the history of the book, especially in Iran and Mughal India. Among the most renowned, special mention must be made of three leaves of the famous *Shah-nameh* (Book of Kings) illustrated at the Jalaraid court in Tabriz in 1335. This masterpiece of world painting was cut apart at the beginning of the century by the antique dealer Charles Demotte.

One year before Migeon's retirement, the Islamic art collection was further enhanced by the bequest of the baroness Salomon de Rothschild, which included, among others, three mosque lamps in enameled and gilded glass from the Mamluk period, metalwork, and a large number of arms, especially Mughal. Migeon also succeeded in getting the Louvre to acquire objects from major collections, such as that of Victor Gay, from which come three little ivory plaques of the Fatimid period.

Upon Migeon's death in 1923, the Islamic section was incorporated into the Asiatic Arts department, which was itself part of the Department of Decorative Arts.

Another great name in the museum

119. *Two ceramic bottles (seventeenth century, Iran, height of the so-called "bottle with a battle of zebus," 31 cm).*

120. *Two rare gobelets in gilded and enameled blown glass, one decorated with figures (the* Goblet with a Horseman, *h. 15.5 cm), the other with geometric motifs. Both of them date, from the mid thirteenth century and come from Syria.*

121. *This bronze incense-burner in the shape of a lion was cast in Khurasan (Iran) in the twelfth century. Gift of David David-Weill, 1933.*

world, and one that was linked with Migeon's, through friendship as well as scholarly publications on Islamic art, is that of Raymond Koechlin. A distinguished medievalist, he was one of the founders of the Friends of the Louvre Society and president of the museum's Artistic Council. His collection, begun in 1895, at the height of Orientalism, included extremely varied works. When it was bequeathed to several museums in 1932, the Louvre's Islamic section received first-rate objects that prove Koechlin's extraordinary taste, from a leaf of Dioscurides's *De materia medica* executed in Baghdad in 1224 to a sixteenth-century masterpiece of the Iznik pottery workshops known as the *Peacock Plate*.

Other names should be cited in this same milieu of curator-collectors. The medievalist J. J. Marquet de Vasselot, for example, was a colleague of Migeon in the Decorative Arts department and a collaborator of Koechlin on scholarly publications. In 1956, his widow was to bequeath the extraordinary little Syrian basin signed by Ibn Zayn, the creator of the "Baptistery of St. Louis," thus giving the Louvre the only known works by this artist. Similarly, the Orientalist archaeologist Georges Salles, grandson of Gustave Eiffel, was a curator in the Asian Arts department and, from 1945 to 1961, director of the Museums of France. He was also a collector with very eclectic tastes, and through him, the Islamic collections were enriched in 1930 with rare ninth-century capitals from northern Syria.

Salles was closely connected with Alphonse Kann, who, in 1935, during his own lifetime, donated one of the most famous works in the world of Islamic art collections: a large ceramic plate from tenth-century Samarkand inscribed with the adage, "The taste of knowledge is bitter in the beginning, but in the end it is sweeter than honey." After Kann's death, his heirs and his executor, Maurice Bokanowski, invited the curators at the Louvre to select pieces for their departments, and in this way five other major ceramics were added to the collections.

There are probably many other donors' names that should be mentioned for this long period between 1890 and 1935: prestigious scholars and archaeologists such as Gaston Maspéro or Léon Schlumberger, other collectors such as J. Matossian and Charles Gillet, or antique dealers such as C. D. Kelekian or C. Kevorkian.

It was in 1937 that a newcomer appeared to the Islamic section at the behest of Georges Salles, who held him in great esteem. This was Jean David-Weill, the master and predecessor of the present writer. An Arabic scholar and a specialist in papyri, he was a man whose vast culture was equaled only by his modesty. His father, David David-Weill, president of the Artistic Council of the Union of National Museums, devoted a large part of his fortune to philanthropic activities and the creation of an enormous collection. All the departments of the Louvre, but also a large number of other museums in Paris and elsewhere in France, benefited from his extreme generosity. His son Jean, who had returned in 1936 from Cairo, where he was a resident at the French Institute for Oriental Archaeology, replaced the Orientalist scholar Gaston Wiet at the Ecole du Louvre in 1937. He was appointed assistant curator under Georges Salles in 1938 and also participated at that time in the major exhibition at the Bibliothèque Nationale devoted to "The Arts of Iran, Ancient Persia, and Baghdad." After five years of refuge in the Free Zone during the German Occupation, he returned to Paris in 1945 and was appointed curator of the Islamic section, now administered with the Oriental Antiquities department but still maintaining its own inventories and complete autonomy in its research. This change of status was confirmed in 1949 with the opening of a new "Muslim gallery" in the palace's central hall (which was in fact the former chapel). Certain gifts and bequests to the Louvre's Oriental collections were yet to come, notably those of Count François Chandon de Briailles, politician and historian of the Latin East, the industrialist Claudius Côte, and the antique dealer Nicolas Landau. But from now on, these collections were enlarged above all through acquisitions on the art market and government preemptions in their favor at Customs or at public auctions. With the support of the great scholar Louis Massignon, Jean David-Weill filled in a large part of the gaps in the area of medieval Iranian art, now one of the best represented in the Louvre. During his lifetime he donated several objects from Egypt to the museum, and in 1972, his bequest con-

123

122-123. *One of the most precious treasures from the Louvre's Islamic art collection: the great so-called "Mantes" carpet. Woven in northwestern Iran at the end of the sixteenth century, it takes its name from the treasury of the Collegiate Church of Mantes where it was formerly housed (detail, the entire carpet measures 783 × 379 cm). Another treasure: the ivory pyxis of al-Mughira dated 968 A.D. (h. 15 cm, Cordoba).*

124

125

126

siderably enhanced the collection of eighth- and ninth-century Egyptian woodwork.

This shift in the acquisitions policy initiated after the Second World War has only been accentuated over the past thirty years. Most of the great collections from the beginning of the century have disappeared, and some of them have even been been spirited out of France illegally in order to enrich the collections of museums in Kuwait or Washington, D.C. At the same time, more specialized collections are now beginning to be constituted. Bequests and gifts have become rare, although mention must be made of Yedda Godard, wife of the architect André Godard, who was director-general of the French Archaeological Services in Iran from 1928 to 1960, as well as the enlightened Paris antique dealers Joseph Soustiel and his son Jean, Ahmet Benli, and Joseph Uzan.

The Paris market has been dethroned by those of London and New York and prices have often become prohibitive, but every year a few handsome objects make their way into the collection of the Islamic section, sometimes through the generosity of the Friends of the Louvre Society. When this is possible, we attempt to find pieces with "pedigrees," as is the case with the miniatures from the Gonse collection, the metalwork and textiles formerly belonging to Gaston Wiet, and the ceramics of Gamsaragam Bey that have been acquired in recent years.

Since 1971, when the room devoted to Islamic art was closed, the works have been exhibited only in three tiny rooms of the Oriental Antiquities department and on the occasion of various exhibitions of greater or lesser stature. After some twenty years of quasi-clandestine existence, the opening of a real section will allow the public to rediscover this art, which so fascinated the great collectors, and painters exactly a century ago at the time of the first "Muslim Art" exhibition.   M. B.-T.

124. *This basin of hammered brass with carved decoration inlaid with silver and gold, was made in Syria or Egypt around 1300. Known as the "Baptistry of St. Louis," (d. 50.5 cm, detail).*

125. *The "Plate of Knowledge," Iran, tenth or eleventh century (d. 37.5 cm).*

126. *Group of ivory and wood carvings from the Fatimid period (Egypt, eleventh-twelfth century).*

127. *A marble tombstone from Egypt dated 877; in front of it, a blown-glass bottle found in the excavations of Susa (Iran, eighth-ninth century, h. 13.5 cm) and the Pomegranate Plate (second half of the ninth century).*

127

PRACTICAL INFORMATION

Access

Subway: Palais-Royal/Musée du Louvre station.

Main Entrance: Pyramid (in the Cour Napoléon).

Other Entrances: Through the Louvre Carrousel (direct access from the subway and the Tuileries); through the Jaujard Gate, and through the Passage Richelieu.

Hours: Daily except Tuesdays, 9 a.m. to 6 p.m. Open evenings until 9:45 p.m. on Mondays for the Richelieu wing and Wednesdays for the all museum.

General Information:
Tel. (331) 40 20 51 51 and 40 20 53 17.
Minitel: 3615 Louvre (24 hours a day).

Admission Fees

Uniform fee: 40 F until 3 p.m., 20 F after 3 p.m. and Sundays.

activities (which galleries are open, special programs, guided tours)
• hosts and hostesses offering multilingual assistance (ten different languages) at the computerized information desk
• annual and quarterly programs describing the museum's activities in detail.

Services for Handicapped Visitors

Nearly all of the Richelieu wing is accessible to visitors with reduced mobility. Elevators and special equipment have been installed in many areas of the Denon and Sully wings. A guide indicating itineraries for visitors with reduced mobility is also available.

Guided tours for groups with reduced mobility or the vision-impaired can be organized by reservation. Tel. (331) 40 20 54 32 and 40 20 58 76.

THE FRIENDS OF THE LOUVRE SOCIETY

In 1897, when government grants for the museum's acquisitions seemed quite limited, a group of art-lovers came together to found the Friends of the Louvre Society. For nearly a hundred years, the society, which now has some forty thousand members, has been assisting the Louvre in its purchases. Thus, through the enlightened suggestions of its board members, the Department of Painting has been enhanced with masterpieces such as the *Avignon Pietà* (1905) and Georges de La Tour's *St. Sebastian* (1981). Similarly, the Decorative Arts department recently gained the empress Eugénie's crown.

Society members have free access to the museum. The different membership categories include: Member (220 F yearly), Supporting Member (500 F), Patron (3,500 F). For information: (331) 40.20.53.74.

Free for certain categories (under 18, teachers, etc.).

Possibility of combined tickets for permanent collections and exhibits.

A "Carte musées et monuments" allows direct access to certain monuments and the permanent collections of many Paris museums. This pass can be purchased in participating institutions or in the Paris subway stations.

Visitor Information

Available in the reception area of the Hall Napoléon (under the Pyramid) are:
• a free guide in six languages
• fifteen video monitors displaying up-to-the-minute information on the day's

A special Minitel-equipped telephone number has been set up for reserving guided tours for the hearing-impaired: (331) 40 20 44 81.

Guided Tours

Individuals:
Tickets are available at the Group Reception Area under the Pyramid, where participants should assemble fifteen minutes before the beginning of the tour. Information: (331) 40 20 52 09.

Guided tours generally last an hour and a half. There are no tours on Tuesdays and Sundays. General tours are conducted in French twice a day and in English three to six times a day depending on

Fold-Out Plan ▶

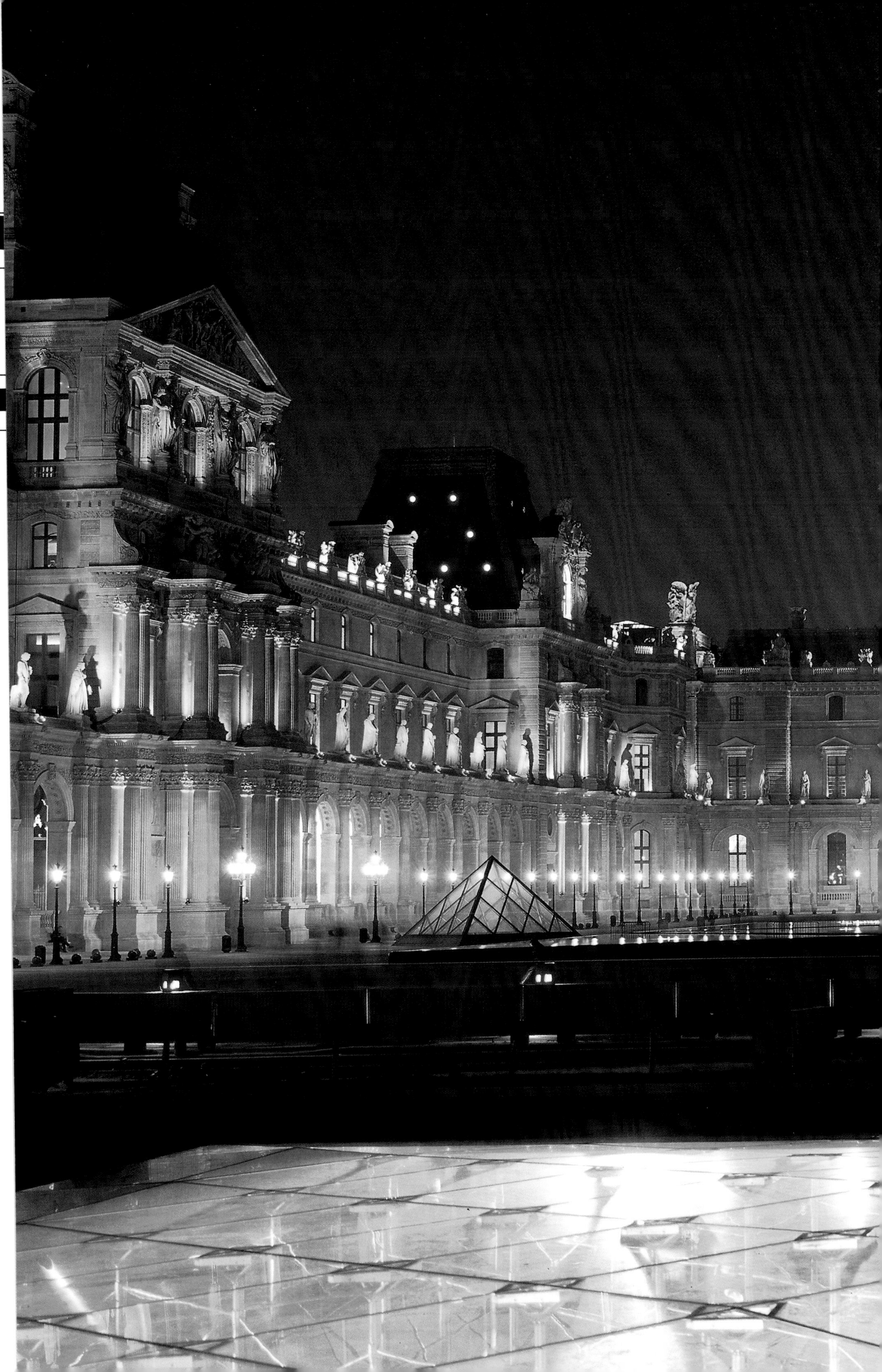

Conception : Agence Anatome

the time of the year. Specialized tours are conducted in French only. Detailed quarterly programs are available in the reception area.
Groups:
Museum guides are available for groups of up to thirty people (daily except Tuesday, Sunday, and holidays). Reservations: (331) 40 20 51 77. There may be a significant waiting period.

Groups
Groups are permitted in the museum every day except Tuesday, Sunday after 1 p.m., and holidays provided that a reservation is made in advance *(all groups must reserve, regardless of whether they are accompanied by a guide or not).*
Tel. (331) 40 20 57 60 (M-F 9:30 a.m.-5:30 p.m.). Fax (331) 40 20 58 24

Workshops
The museum's workshops are intended to give participants of all ages (5 years and up) the possibility of actively acquiring a better understanding of works of art. They are led by art historians or artists and last two or two and a half hours. Examples of topics include: Egyptian costumes, filming works of art, the expression of feelings.
Information and reservations (should be made in the morning for the afternoon): (331) 40 20 52 63.

Temporary Exhibitions
Nearly a dozen temporary exhibits are held each year in the different areas of the museum:
● in the Hall Napoléon (under the Pyramid)

● in the Richelieu wing, a new exibition gallery south of the Marly courtyard, on the entresol
● in the Flore pavilion, second floor

The Auditorium
The 420-seat auditorium is used for concerts, films, talks, and conferences. Information: (331) 40 20 51 86

Films
Films on art that have been produced by the Louvre are shown every day (except Tuesday) in the two projection rooms in the Hall Napoléon (under the Pyramid). Screenings are held at 11 a.m., 12:30, 2, 3:30, and 5 p.m., with an additional screening at 6:30 p.m. on Mondays and Wednesdays. Admission is free.

Restaurants
Under the Pyramid
Le Grand Louvre restaurant (reception level), open noon to midnight. Tel. (331) 40 20 53 41
Café du Louvre (reception level), open from 9 a.m. to 10 p.m.
Cafétéria du Musée (mezzanine), open from 11:45 a.m. to 3 p.m.
Café Napoléon (mezzanine), open from 10:30 a.m. to 7 p.m.
Denon Wing
Café Mollien, Denon 9, open 9 a.m. to 5 p.m. and until 8 p.m. on late nights.
Richelieu Wing
Café Richelieu, Richelieu 2
Café Marly, on the ground floor, open 9 a.m. to 2 a.m. daily. Entry from outside the museum (Cour Napoléon) only.

128. *An impressive demonstration of the importance of the Friends of the Louvre Society's gifts: the* Avignon Pietà *by Enguerrand Quarton (wood panel, 163 x 218 cm).*

129. *The Cour Napoleon with I.M. Pei's Pyramid as it was lit by Électricité de France for the inauguration ceremonies in November 1993.*

130. *Next double page: the bookshop of the Louvre.*

Like an echo of the Pyramid that marks the entrance to the Louvre, I. M. Pei has designed an inverted pyramid illuminating the heart of the vast shopping mall located between the museum proper and the parking areas. The idea of Michel Macary, who is in charge of the project, was provide a logical and uninterrupted extension of the reception areas under the Cour Napoléon. With the same quality of conception and execution that characterizes all the work of I. M. Pei and his team, a monumental space is associated with the extreme refinement of the building materials.
The Louvre Carrousel, managed and constructed by the SARI investment group (Générale des Eaux 65%, Lucia 35%), is intended as a shopping mall and first-rate conference site. Essential services such as a pharmacy, bank,

THE LOUVRE CARROUSEL

currency exchange center, and restaurants, but also perfume shops, gift shops, and above all, a megastore devoted mainly to music will fill the 8,300 square meters of the mall, which will be convenient to museum visitors and directly accessible from the subway.
The conference area, occupying 7,500 square meters, includes four multifunction rooms designed by Gérard Grandval; these can hold up to 1,700 people for conferences, exhibitions, or fashion shows (which were previously held in tents set up in the Cour Carrée).
As an underground thoroughfare, the Louvre Carrousel is at once an extension of the museum and totally independent of it, a space for relaxation and entertainment intended to attract not only the tourists visiting the museum but the Parisian public as well.

BOOKSHOP

In 1989, when the Louvre bookshop moved into the new space designed for it under the Pyramid by Jean-Michel Wilmotte, the challenge was formidable. Indeed, it was no longer to serve simply as a museum bookshop—the change was already underway—but to become a real art bookshop. And if possible, the very best one in Paris.

Four years later, it is clear that the goal has been reached. Alongside the ever-growing numbers of guides and catalogues are more than twenty thousand publications in French and other languages, from the most luxurious editions to paperbacks, on subjects ranging from painting, sculpture, and architecture to aesthetics and the history of art. Plus the specialized magazines. All of which is divided between shelves and tables that allow for browsing. The staff, headed first by Marc Plocki and now by Marie-France Langlois, has proven that the Louvre can offer more than other bookshops.

There is no need to look for a children's section. It occupies a virtual bookshop of its own on the mezzanine, where some of the most inventive titles are to be found, providing a true delight for young and old alike. The only regret is that it is not yet sufficiently well known.

The mezzanine level also contains the gifts section, which offers visitors everything from a cast of the *Venus de Milo* to replicas of Egyptian or Etruscan jewelry to tee-shirts, scarves, and other accessories. Plus the engravings section, with its stock of proofs made from the copperplates of the masters. Those who are in a hurry will be pleased to know that they can acquire guides and postcards as they dash through the galleries, since sales desks have been placed along the route. And the forgetful need not worry any longer: they can do the same on the way back to the parking lot, thanks to the RMN (Union of National Museums) shop inside the Louvre Carrousel.

Finally, the big news for the end of 1993 was the opening of a postcard shop also designed by Jean-Michel Wilmotte. It brings together nearly two thousand images of works in the Louvre and other museums in France, one of the largest selections of its kind.   □

The retail outlets of the RMN at the Louvre, main bookshop, access through the Pyramid. Daily except Tuesdays, 9:30 a.m.-9:30 p.m. Tel. 40 20 50 50.

130

bijoux...cadeaux...moulages...bijoux...cadeaux...moulages...bijoux...cadeaux...m

THE LOUVRE BY NIGHT

Illuminating a venerable French landmark on the occasion of its bicentennial was a singular task that called for highlighting a monument with moderation, subtlety, and sensitivity. This was the challenge taken up by the Electricity Company of France (Électricité de France) for the "lighting design" of the Louvre's Cour Carrée. In order to obtain the best result, the company's researchers used computer models to test the different kinds of lighting virtually before turning to trials on the building itself.

From dusk to darkness, a veil of light was to progressively envelop this part of the palace without distorting it. But at the same time, the projectors could not disfigure the facade during the day. The alliance of aesthetics, efficiency, and economy of energy was thus a central requirement for the project. The research undertaken allowed the perfecting of a system of lighting from above integrating lamps with long-life xenon bulbs (twenty thousand hours). In addition, the system was equipped with intensity variators allowing the building to "breathe" in light.

During the inauguration of the Richelieu wing, the Electric Company of France is offering visitors an "itinerary in light" from the Institute to the gardens of the Palais-Royal that will bring out of the night the wonders of the statuary in the Cour Carrée and the Richelieu wing.

After the Mont St. Michel and now the illumination of the Cour Carrée, the Electric Company of France will continue to participate in major operations renewing France's patrimony at home and abroad. □

Acknowledgments

Connaissance des Arts would like to express its gratitude to those who have partipated in the creation of this special issue. Above all to Michel Laclotte, president-director of the Louvre Museum, and Jean Lebrat, president of the Public Authority for the Grand Louvre, as well as the curators in charge of the different departments, Daniel Alcouffe, Marthe Bernus-Taylor, Annie Caubet, Jean-René Gaborit, Alain Pasquier, Pierre Rosenberg, and Françoise Viatte, all of whom have facilitated our staff's access to the collections.

We should also like to recognize the contributions of Catherine Belanger, Françoise Mardrus, and Patricia Mounier, as well as those of Elisabeth Fontan, Jacques Foucart, Bernadette Letellier, Sophie Guillot de Suduiraut, Elise Thiebaut, and all the staff of the Anatome company.

Finally, our thanks to Jean-François Chougnet, Anne de Margerie, and Marc Plocki. And of course, to Stephen Rustow of Pei Cobb Freed and to Yann Weymouth.

131. *A detail showing the "lighting design" of the Horloge pavilion on the Cour Carrée side. Built after 1624, the pavilion was decorated in large part by the sculptor Jacques Sarrazin.*

CONNAISSANCE DES ARTS Numéro hors série. **RÉDACTEUR EN CHEF :** Philip JODIDIO. **RESPONSABLE :** Virginie de LA BATUT. **SECRÉTARIAT DE RÉDACTION :** Françoise FOULON. **DOCUMENTATION :** Sylvie BLIN. **SERVICE PHOTOS :** Martine JOSSE. **SECRÉTARIAT :** Inès DUVAL, Monique FOUQUET, Kathryn LEVESQUE. **MAQUETTE :** Sylvie CHESNAY. **ONT COLLABORÉ À CE NUMÉRO :** Jacques TOUBON, ministre de la Culture et de la Francophonie - Et Daniel ALCOUFFE, Marthe BERNUS-TAYLOR, Annie CAUBET, Bruno FOUCART, Michel LACLOTTE, Jean LEBRAT, Denis PICARD. **DIRECTION TECHNIQUE :** Christian LECOCQ. **SERVICE COMMERCIAL :** Philippe THOMAS. **TRADUCTION :** Miriam ROSEN.

COUVERTURE ET PAGES : 8, 36-7, 42 milieu, 45, 52 (2, 3, 5), 53 : Alfred Wolf. Pages : 4-5 : Arnaud Carpentier, Stéphane Couturier/Archipress, RMN, Alfred Wolf. Pages : 7, 13, 14, 15, 25, 27, 28-9, 31 dr., 32 g., 34, 35, 42 bas, 43, 71 ht, 76 bas, 78, 79, 84, 85, 86, 90 bas, 91, 93 : Roger Guillemot - Bernard Saint-Genès. Pages : 10, 11, 12, 16 (1, 2, 3), 18-9, 20, 22, 23, 24, 26 milieu et bas, 28 haut et milieu, 32 dr. et bas, 39, 55, 57, 59, 60, 62, 66, 69, 92, 94, 98, 99, 100 milieu, 102 : RMN. Page : 16 bas : Bibliothèque nationale, Paris. Pages : 21, 46, 47, 72, 82 : Stéphane Couturier/Archipress. Pages : 24 dr. et bas, 26 ht et dr., 26 g., 28 bas, 31 g, 32 dr. et ht : Jacqueline Guillot. Pages : 29 dr., 33, 40, 41, 44, 48-9, 51, 54, 56, 58, 61, 62-3, 64-5, 67, 68-9, 70, 71 bas, 73, 74-5, 76 ht et milieu, 77, 81, 83, 87, 89, 90 ht et milieu, 95, 96-7, 100 ht et bas, 101, 108-9 : Arnaud Carpentier. Pages : 38, 42 ht, 52 (4 et 5) : Marc Riboud. Page : 52 (1) : Deidi von Schaewen. Pages : 105-6 : Photothèque EDF - Claude Pauquet. Page : 111 : Photothèque EDF - Jean-Marc Charles.

© 1993 Société Française de Promotion Artistique, 25 rue de Ponthieu, 75008 Paris. Tél. 43 59 62 00. R.C. Paris 75 B 4306 Seine. Direction de la publication : C. Lecocq - Commission paritaire : 55084 - ISSN 1242-9198 - Dépôt légal : 4e trimestre 1993 - Imprimé et composé par ISTRA-BL Strasbourg - Photogravure : Clin d'œil, Vanves et Cliché-Union, Montrouge.